To A Fellow Kansan
Terrance Tice

Best Wishes,
Marguerite Mitchell Marshall
9/11/82

Eva Geary
Sept 13, 1982

FIRST EDITION

All rights reserved, including the right of
reproduction in whole or in part in any form.

Copyright © 1982 by Marguerite Mitchell Marshall

Published by Vantage Press, Inc.
516 West 34th Street, New York, New York 10001

ISBN: 533-04190-2

Library of Congress Catalog Card No.: 79-62940

In Memorium

Mr. Henry Levi Mitchell (1887–1971)
Mrs. Emily Fonchoser Mitchell (1890–1973)

To My Family

Mr. Cecil Mitchell, Brother
Mrs. Genevieve Mitchell Shedrick, Sister
Mrs. Ida Mae Mitchell Yolkum, Sister
Mr. Ulysses Marshall, Husband

In-Laws

Mrs. Darlene Adkins Mitchell
Mr. Wilbur Shedrick
Mr. William Yolkum
Mr. Thomas and Mrs. Edna Coachman

Niece and Nephew

Mr. Benjamin and Mrs. Antoinette Brown
(and Daughters, Knachia and Emileta Brown)

Contents

March on Washington for Jobs and Freedom 1

Poems and Tributes to the Kennedy Family 10

Poems—Dr. Martin Luther King, Jr. 18

The Three Wives 21

Tributes to Members of the Washington, D.C.
    Public School System and Dawson, Georgia 23

Poems 39

Essays 53

People Whom I Admire for the Contribution They Made
    to Our Society 92

THE PATH TO PEACE

March on Washington for Jobs and Freedom

Wednesday, August 28, 1963

The people came to Washington, D.C., for the "March On Washington," via trains, airplanes, buses, and automobiles, and some walked. It is estimated that 250 Virginians walked; they were led by the "Freedom Fighters" from Danville, Virginia.

Others, also, trudged from nearby East Coast areas: New York, New Jersey, Delaware, Maryland, and the Carolinas. By 11:00 A.M. over 250,000 people had assembled at the Washington Monument.

While this assembling was taking place, Dr. Martin Luther King, Jr., A. Philip Randolph, Rabbi Joachim Prinz, Whitney Young, Jr., Walter Reuther, and Roy Wilkins were meeting on Capitol Hill. They had a conference with Senators Mike Mansfield and Everett Dirksen, House Speaker John McCormack, and Representative Charles Halleck to discuss the Civil Rights legislation. This meeting adjourned around 10:30 A.M., and the delegation arrived at the Washington Monument about 10:45 A.M.

At the Washington Monument, from 6:00 A.M. until 10:45 A.M., we were entertained by television, motion picture and Broadway stars, also other notables. The list is long, but I shall attempt to name a few. Sammy Davis, Jr., was the master of ceremonies. He called on the following performers to enliven the audience: Joan Baez, Josephine Baker from Paris, France, Bobby Darin, Jackie Robinson, Dick Gregory, Odetta, Sidney Poitier, Lena Horne, Ossie Davis and Ruby Dee,

MARCH ON WASHINGTON FOR JOBS AND FREEDOM
AUGUST 28, 1963

LINCOLN MEMORIAL PROGRAM

1. The National Anthem — *Led by* Marian Anderson.
2. Invocation — The Very Rev. Patrick O'Boyle, *Archbishop of Washington.*
3. Opening Remarks — A. Philip Randolph, *Director March on Washington for Jobs and Freedom.*
4. Remarks — Dr. Eugene Carson Blake, *Stated Clerk, United Presbyterian Church of the U.S.A.; Vice Chairman, Commission on Race Relations of the National Council of Churches of Christ in America.*
5. Tribute to Negro Women Fighters for Freedom — Mrs. Medgar Evers
   - Daisy Bates
   - Diane Nash Bevel
   - Mrs. Medgar Evers
   - Mrs. Herbert Lee
   - Rosa Parks
   - Gloria Richardson
6. Remarks — John Lewis, *National Chairman, Student Nonviolent Coordinating Committee.*
7. Remarks — Walter Reuther, *President, United Automobile, Aerospace and Agricultural Implement Wokers of America, AFL-CIO; Chairman, Industrial Union Department, AFL-CIO.*
8. Remarks — James Farmer, *National Director, Congress of Racial Equality.*
9. Selection — Eva Jessye *Choir*
10. Prayer — Rabbi Uri Miller, *President Synagogue Council of America.*
11. Remarks — Whitney M. Young, Jr., *Executive Director, National Urban League.*
12. Remarks — Mathew Ahmann, *Executive Director, National Catholic Conference for Interracial Justice.*
13. Remarks — Roy Wilkins, *Executive Secretary, National Association for the Advancement of Colored People.*
14. Selection — Miss Mahalia Jackson
15. Remarks — Rabbi Joachim Prinz, *President American Jewish Congress.*
16. Remarks — The Rev. Dr. Martin Luther King, Jr., *President, Southern Christian Leadership Conference.*
17. The Pledge — A Philip Randolph
18. Benediction — Dr. Benjamin E. Mays, *President, Morehouse College.*

"WE SHALL OVERCOME"

Statement by the heads of the ten organizations calling for discipline in connection with the Washington March of August 28, 1963:

"The Washington March of August 28th is more than just a demonstration.

"It was conceived as an outpouring of the deep feeling of millions of white and colored American citizens that the time has come for the government of the United States of America, and particularly for the Congress of that government, to grant and guarantee complete equality in citizenship to the Negro minority of our population.

"As such, the Washington March is a living petition—in the flesh—of the scores of thousands of citizens of both races who will be present from all parts of our country.

"It will be orderly, but not subservient. It will be proud, but not arrogant. It will be non-violent, but not timid. It will be unified in purposes and behavior, not splintered into groups and individual competitors. It will be outspoken, but not raucous.

"It will have the dignity befitting a demonstration in behalf of the human rights of twenty millions of people, with the eye and the judgment of the world focused upon Washington, D.C., on August 28, 1963.

"In a neighborhood dispute there may be stunts, rough words and even hot insults; but when a whole people speaks to its government, the dialogue and the action must be on a level reflecting the worth of that people and the responsibility of that government.

"We, the undersigned, who see the Washington March as wrapping up the dreams, hopes, ambitions, tears, and prayers of millions who have lived for this day, call upon the members, followers and wellwishers of our several organizations to make the March a disciplined and purposeful demonstration.

"We call upon them all, black and white, to resist provocations to disorder and to violence.

"We ask them to remember that evil persons are determined to smear this March and to discredit the cause of equality by deliberate efforts to stir disorder.

"We call for self-discipline, so that no one in our own ranks, however enthusiastic, shall be the spark for disorder.

"We call for resistance to the efforts of those who, while not enemies of the March as such, might seek to use it to advance causes not dedicated primarily to civil rights or to the welfare of our country.

"We ask each and every one in attendance in Washington or in spiritual attendance back home to place the Cause above all else.

"Do not permit a few irresponsible people to hang a new problem around our necks as we return home. Let's do what we came to do—place the national human rights problem squarely on the doorstep of the national Congress and of the Federal Government.

"Let's win at Washington."

SIGNED:

Mathew Ahmann, *Executive Director of the National Catholic Conference for Interracial Justice.*

Reverend Eugene Carson Blake, *Vice-Chairman of the Commission on Race Relations of the National Council of Churches of Christ in America*

James Farmer, *National Director of the Congress of Racial Equality.*

Reverend Martin Luther King, Jr., *President of the Southern Christian Leadership Conference.*

John Lewis, *Chairman of the Student Nonviolent Coordinating Committee.*

Rabbi Joachim Prinz, *President of the American Jewish Congress.*
A. Philip Randolph, *President of the Negro American Labor Council.*
Walter Reuther, *President of the United Automobile, Aerospace and Agricultural Implement Workers of America, AFL-CIO, and Chairman,* Industrial Union Department, AFL-CIO.
Roy Wilkins, *Executive Secretary of the National Association for the Advancement of Colored People.*
Whitney M. Young, Jr., *Executive Director of the National Urban League.*

In addition, the March has been endorsed by major religious, fraternal, labor and civil rights organizations. A full list, too long to include here, will be published.

WHAT WE DEMAND*

1. Comprehensive and effective *civil rights legislation* from the present Congress—without compromise or filibuster—to guarantee all Americans
   - access to all public accommodations
   - decent housing
   - adequate and integrated education
   - the right to vote

2. Withholding of Federal funds from all programs in which discrimination exists.

3. *Desegregation of all school districts in 1963.*

4. Enforcement of the *Fourteenth Amendment*—reducing Congressional representation of states where citizens are disfranchised.

5. A new *Executive Order* banning discrimination in all housing supported by federal funds.

6. Authority for the Attorney General to institute *injunctive suits* when any constitutional right is violated.

7. A massive federal program to train and place all unemployed workers—Negro and white—on meaningful and dignified jobs at decent wages.

8. A national *minimum wage* act that will give all Americans a decent standard of living. (Government surveys show that anything less than $2.00 an hour fails to do this.)

9. A broadened *Fair Labor Standards Act* to include all areas of employment which are presently excluded.

10. A federal *Fair Employment Practices Act* barring discrimination by federal, state, and municipal governments, and by employers, contractors, employment agencies, and trade unions.

---

*Support of the March does not necessarily indicate endorsement of every demand listed. Some organizations have not had an opportunity to take an official position on all of the demands advocated here.

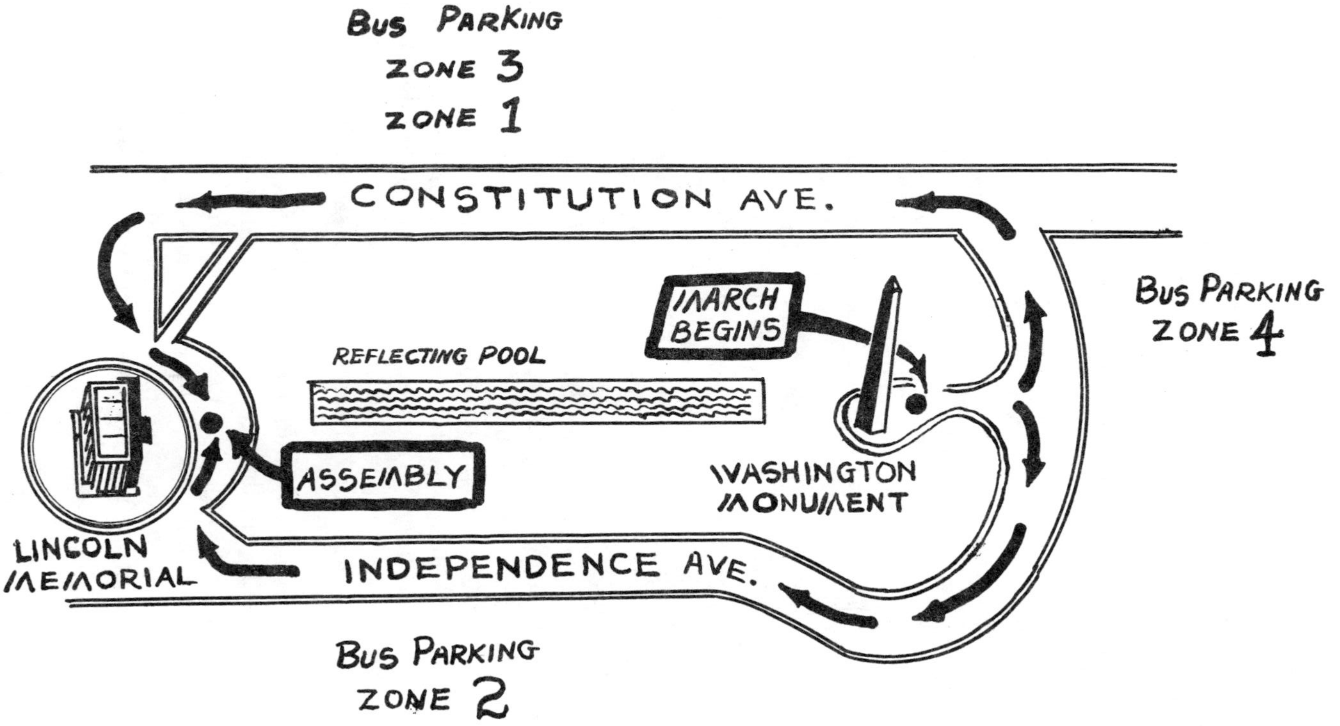

BUS PARKING
ZONE 3
ZONE 1

CONSTITUTION AVE.

MARCH BEGINS

REFLECTING POOL

WASHINGTON MONUMENT

ASSEMBLY

INDEPENDENCE AVE.

LINCOLN MEMORIAL

BUS PARKING
ZONE 4

BUS PARKING
ZONE 2

Charlton Heston, Harry Belafonte, Diahann Carroll, Paul Newman, Mahalia Jackson, Josh White, and others. Burt Lancaster, who also came in from Paris, France, brought a scroll containing 150 signatures of artists of all nationalities conveying congratulations and success. We listened to the music, prayers, and speeches during this period.

George W. Collins, writing in the Washington *Afro-American* newspaper on August 31, 1963 (p. 6), stated that, "Many had known no sleep for hours. Thousands were feet weary. Others were tired. But tiredness found no comfort in the ranks of the marchers. Their hearts, minds, soul and spirits soared on the magic wings of freedom and they marched with dignity, pride and purpose."

The march started at 11:00 A.M. There were two sections in order that the movement to the Lincoln Memorial would not run over an hour. At the head of the march, going the Constitution Avenue route to the Lincoln Memorial, were Dr. Martin Luther King Jr., Mr. A. Philip Randolph, Mr. Roy Wilkins, Mr. Walter Reuther, Mr. Whitney Young, Jr., Mr. Mathew Ahmann, Dr. Eugene C. Blake, Rabbi Joachim Prinz, Mr. John Lewis, Mr. Floyd McKissac, Dr. Ralph Bunche, and Reverend Joseph Rauh. Each line, locked arm in arm with each other, marched along singing freedom songs. The exceptions to arm and hand locking were those carrying pennants, banners, and posters. At the head of the route going the Independence Avenue route were Rabbi Uri Miller, Jackie Robinson, Sammy Davis, Jr., the Freedom Fighters, and others. This section arrived early and went to the platform to perform for the audience already assembled. Peter, Paul and Mary were rendering ballads when we reached the Lincoln Memorial.

At the Lincoln Memorial, the audience stood, while those appearing on the program were seated on the platform to be near the lectern. The program opening was the singing of the national anthem, led by Miss Camilla Williams in lieu of Miss Anderson, who had not yet arrived. Then the invocation was given by The Very Reverend Patrick O'Boyle, archbishop of Washington. We listened intently to the remarks by A. Philip Randolph, John Lewis, Walter Reuther, Roy Wilkins, and the tribute to Negro Women Fighters for Freedom by Mrs. Medgar Evers' proxy. The selections by the Dr. Eva Jessye Choir were very touching. By this time, many relaxed and sat on the grass to listen to the remaining program. When Miss Mahalia Jackson sang a medley of spirtuals, tears were in evidence all around you. Rabbi Uri Miller offered prayer, followed by the remarks of Whitney Young, Jr., and Mathew Ahmann. Miss Marian Anderson sang "He's Got the Whole World in His Hands." After remarks by Rabbi Joachim Prinz, Dr. Martin Luther King, Jr., took the lectern. He gave an electrifying speech entitled "I have a Dream." When the people heard this statement, they stood, cheered, and applauded. He held the crowd's attention by proclaiming: "I have a dream that one day on the red hills of Georgia the sons of former slaves and the sons of former slaveowners will sit down together at the table of brotherhood . . . " With this phrase, he received a standing ovation. Mr. A. Philip Randolph inspired the crowd when he proposed "The Pledge." He told us to pledge: I will join and support all actions undertaken in good faith in accord with the time-honored democratic tradition of non-violent protest, of peaceful assembly and petition, and of redress through the courts and the legislative process.

I pledge to carry the message of the march to my friends and neighbors back home and to arouse them to an equal commitment and an equal effort.

I will march and I will write letters. I will demonstrate and I will vote. I will work to make sure that my voice and those of my brothers ring clear and determined from every corner of our land.

I pledge my heart and my mind and my body, unequivocally and without regard to personal sacrifice, to the achievement of social peace through social justice.

Benediction was given by Dr. Benjamin E. Mays, president, Morehouse College, Atlanta, Georgia. At the conclusion of the benediction, the organ played "We Shall Overcome," and the crowd dispersed chanting this freedom song.

Following this ceremony, Dr. Martin Luther King, Jr. and the leaders of the march met with President John F. Kennedy and Vice-President Lyndon B. Johnson at the White House. After an hour inside, they all came out, and President Kennedy issued a statement. He pledged all efforts to increase employment and eliminate discrimination in employment practices. The president stated to the crowd that had gathered:

History has seen many demonstrations of widely varying character and for a whole host of reasons. As our thoughts travel to other demonstrations that have occurred in different parts of the world, this nation can properly be proud of the demonstration that has occurred here today . . . One cannot help but be impressed with the deep fervor and the quiet dignity that characterizes the thousands who have gathered in the Nation's Capitol from across the country.*

Everyone returned home enlivened with a feeling of "being glad to be alive and participate in such a historical event." I am glad that my sister and I, who reside in Washington, D.C., could join the group in its fight for freedom.

The Theme of the March

Jobs (Employment) and Freedom (Civil Rights)

The Chairmen of the March

Mr. A. Philip Randolph, Director of the March
    President of the Negro American Labor Council
    President of the International Brotherhood
        of Sleeping Car Porters and
    Vice-President of the AFL-CIO

---

*"The Day of the Great March," The Washington *Daily News*, August 29, 1963, p. 12, columns 2 and 3.

Poems and Tributes to the Kennedy Family

To a Pioneer

The Flag

> Of the United States,
>> Gracefully moving in a gentle breeze
>> And lowered to half mast
>
> Over the White House in Washington, D.C.
>> As a symbol to the World that:
>
> The President of the United States,
>> John Fitzgerald Kennedy,
>>> is dead.

The Pioneer

> Opened a Twentieth Century Door called
> "The New Frontier."
> Just behind this door, he found and gave
> to the World:
>
>> L I F E
>>
>> Love of humanity
>> Integrity in all we do
>> Freedom from bondage, and
>> Energy to sustain our Democratic
>> way of Life.

Mr. Bayard Rustin, Deputy Director of the March
Executive Secretary of the War Resisters League
Former Field Secretary for the Congress of Racial Equa (CORE)

The Signs, Banners and Posters Carried

1. End Segregated Rules in Public Schools
2. We March for Jobs for All, Now
3. We Demand Voting Rights
4. We Demand F.E.P.C. Laws
5. End Police Brutality
6. We Demand Decent Housing
7. We Demand Equal Rights, Now
8. We Demand First Class Citizenship
9. Home Rule for the District of Columbia
10. We March Together:
    Catholics, Jews, Protestants
    For Dignity and Brotherhood for All Men under God

The Songs

1. "Oh Freedom"
2. "Freedom Riders Ain't Scared . . . "
3. "I've Got a Hammer . . . "
4. "We Shall Overcome"
   —Theme Song of the Civil Rights Movement
5. "Free At Last!"

Now the door is closed.
There is darkness everywhere;
The Pioneer is no longer with us.

The People

Offer solemn prayers and,
    Mourning sorrowfully
Lament the passing of their
    Commander-In-Chief
JOHN FITZGERALD KENNEDY.

A Sonnet to the First Lady

Ecce suus! The First Lady Of Our Land,
Jacqueline Lee Bouvier Kennedy,
Walking behind the caisson of her husband,
The martyred President, John F. Kennedy.

The black veil adorning her face and hat
Did not conceal the teardrop in her eye;
And all around her people breathed a prayer
That she and the children now would unify.

Noon, 25 November, 1963—
The cortege leaves the White House sanctuary
For Mass at St. Matthew's Cathedral—a plea,
Then to Arlington National Cemetery.

With interment complete, she, Edward, and Robert
Ex more, light the Eternal Flame in concert.

Washington, D.C.
November 22, 1963

TO THE JOHN F. KENNEDY CHILDREN:
   Caroline Kennedy and
   John F. Kennedy, Junior

Mon cher petit fille et garçon:

With God's favor, may you forever be safe and secure in this your native homeland. May He continue to guide and protect you.

Always remember the good thoughts and deeds that your parents taught you. Take this knowledge, and upon it build a happy, honest, and wholesome life. Share your talents with humanity as did your family.

When you become a mature woman and man, an eminent and dignified life will be yours. It is befitting that you devote this life to enhancing the principles and the accomplishments your families gave as their legacy.

Yours truly,
Marguerite Mitchell Marshall

The Joseph P. Kennedy family in 1938. From left are: (seated) Eunice, Jean, Edward (on lap of his father), Joseph P. Kennedy, Patricia, and Kathleen; (standing) Rosemary, Robert, John, Mrs. Rose Kennedy, and Joseph, Jr. (Joseph, Jr. was killed in action as a Navy pilot in World War II; Kathleen was killed in a plane crash in France in 1948; John was assassinated while serving as U.S. president in 1963; and Robert was assassinated during the 1968 Democratic presidential primary campaign.)

Washington, D.C.
November 24, 1963

TO THE JOSEPH P. KENNEDY FAMILY:
    Mr. Joseph P. Kennedy, Sr.
    Mrs. Rose Kennedy and
    The Sisters and Brothers

My dear Mr. and Mrs. J. P. Kennedy and Family:

The people of the world loved and needed your son, John Fitzgerald Kennedy, as did each of you.
We loved him because he:

> understood the problems of all ethnic groups;
> gave so generously of himself;
> was enthusiastic about life.

We needed him because he:

> enacted legislation that enhanced our
>   country's welfare;
> envisioned a world of peace
>   and good will among men;
> had the ability to satisfy our needs.

For the love he gave so generously, we are reverent.
For the need he had to belong to the world, we are grateful. We shall always cherish his memory.

                              Yours truly,
                        Marguerite Mitchell Marshall

MEMORIAL SERVICE

FOR OUR MARTYRED PRESIDENT

JOHN F. KENNEDY

On the final day of national mourning

Sunday, December 22, 1963 — 4:00 P.M.

at the Lincoln Memorial, Washington, D. C.

Memorial Music	Howard University Choir, Dean Warner Lawson, Conductor
	U.S. Army Band, Col. Hugh Curry, Conductor
Our National Anthem	Choir and Assembly
Opening Remarks	Bishop John Wesley Lord, Co-Chairman, Interreligious Committee on Race Relations
Invocation	Bishop Smallwood E. Williams
Navy Hymn	Howard University Choir
Memorial Prayer for President Kennedy	Bishop William F. Creighton
Prayer for Our Country and its Leaders	Rabbi Lewis A. Weintraub

Candlelighting Ceremony

"The energy, the faith, the devotion which we bring to this endeavor will light our country and all who serve it, and the glow from that fire can truly light the world."
John F. Kennedy, Inaugural Address

Prayer for Brotherhood	Msgr. John S. Spence
Address	The President of the United States
Benediction	Dr. E. Franklin Jackson
America The Beautiful	Choir and Assembly

AMERICA THE BEAUTIFUL

O Beautiful for spacious skies,
For amber waves of grain,
For purple mountain majesties
Above the fruited plain!
America! America!
God shed His grace on thee,
And crown thy good with brotherhood
From sea to shining sea!

O beautiful for pilgrim feet,
Whose stern, impassioned stress,
A thoroughfare for freedom beat
Across the wilderness!
America! America!
God mend thine every flaw,
Confirm thy soul in self-control,
Thy liberty in law!

O beautiful for patriot dream
That sees beyond the years,
Thine alabaster cities gleam,
Undimmed by human tears!
America! America!
God shed His grace on thee,
And crown thy good with brotherhood
From sea to shining sea!

★ ★ ★

SPONSORING ORGANIZATIONS

INTERRELIGIOUS COMMITTEE ON RACE RELATIONS
Washington, D. C.

Chairman

The Most Rev. Patrick A. O'Boyle, D.D.

Co-Chairmen

The Right Rev. William F. Creighton, D.D.
Bishop John Wesley Lord, D.D.

Rabbi Lewis A. Weintraub
Bishop Smallwood E. Williams, D.D.

★ ★ ★

CATHOLIC ARCHDIOCESE OF WASHINGTON
The Most Rev. Patrick A. O'Boyle, D.D., Archbishop

★ ★ ★

COUNCIL OF CHURCHES OF GREATER WASHINGTON

The Rev. David G. Colwell
President

The Rev. Virgil E. Lowder, D.D.
Executive Director

★ ★ ★

JEWISH COMMUNITY COUNCIL OF GREATER WASHINGTON

Richard K. Lyon, *President*   Isaac Franck, *Executive Director*

The Accused

The deed is done,
And they say
    Lee Harvey Oswald is the one
Who committed this ghastly crime.
I wonder what was on his mind,
When he pulled the trigger
    without a blink.
Did he stop to think
That this human being had a goal?
Now it is too late to think.
The deed is done.
The deed is done.

A Tribute to Senator Robert F. Kennedy
On the Occasion of His Death by an Assassin, June 5, 1968

    This—
Righteous young man, during his lifetime, maintained
Open-minded views of world affairs.
    His—
Benevolent and charitable disposition toward humanity,
Enthusiastic pursuit of improving our democratic
    system of government, and
Reliable facts on oppression, depredation, and
    injustice, attest to his
Truthful way of living.
    He was—
Faithful to his Country, to God, and to Man.
    He did bequeath:
Kindness to your fellow-man.
Energy to sustain our way of life.
National unity to build a solid world.
Nobleness of purposes.
Ethical values at all times.
Dignity of actions and deeds, and a
Yearning for a great nation.

Poems—
Dr. Martin Luther King, Jr.

The Black Moses: The Reverend Dr. Martin Luther King, Jr.

Negroes in America
    received another defeat
        in their search for Freedom
    with the assassination of the
Reverend Dr. Martin Luther King, Jr.

Through his Philosophy
    of nonviolence:
        The doors of integration and
            equal opportunities opened
            for Negroes.
        Civil Rights Laws became a reality
            and gave us insight into justice

Throughout his Life
    which was a symbol of Hope, Love,
        Truth, and Freedom for all mankind:
        He led us out of the wilderness
            where despair, hatred, and
            strife were prevalent.

Through his Legacy
>   He left us the " . . . dream that
>   one day . . . the sons of former
>   slaves and the sons of former
>   slave owners will be able to
>   sit down together at the table
>   of brotherhood."

Now the Negro must take this legacy
>   that he left and build a firm
>   foundation for the future.
>   Thus assuring his reaching the
>   Promised Land where a better life
>   for humanity is reserved.

To the King Children

Dear Martin Luther King, III, Yolanda King, Bernice King, and Dexter King:

    Always remember the love and devotion that your father gave you. Also remember that it was your father's wish for you to grow in wisdom and understanding.

    To grow in wisdom will inspire you to follow the "Golden Rule." While growing in understanding will help you to see the good in all mankind.

Yours truly,
Marguerite M. Marshall

The Man Who Had a Dream
by Antoinette Yolkum*

A man of non-violence,
A man of peace,
A man who gave his life for his
    followers, who in turn must
    carry on with the "Dream."
A man who was to lead us to the
    Promised Land where
        Righteousness, Love and
        Freedom abound.
A man who struggled daily
    to bring mankind together
    to aid the downtrodden, and
    to effect a brotherhood society—
This man was
    THE REVEREND DR. MARTIN LUTHER KING, JR.

---

*A student attending McKinley High School, Washington D.C., 1968

The Three Wives

The Three Wives

Here the three women stand—
    Mrs. Jacqueline B. Kennedy, wife
        of the martyred President of the
        United States,
    JOHN F. KENNEDY;
    Mrs. Coretta Scott King, wife
        of the Crusader for Civil Rights,
        Founder and President of the
        Southern Christian Leadership
        Conference, and recipient of
        the Nobel Peace Prize,
    DR. MARTIN LUTHER KING, JR.;
    Mrs. Ethel S. Kennedy, wife
        of the Great Humanitarian, former
        Senator (Democrat) from New York, and
        Attorney General of the United States,
    ROBERT F. KENNEDY:
with heads bowed and asking for guidance from above.

    As their husbands fought and died for the cause of justice, these three women had one thing in common: they must suffer in silence. The world mourns with them. Now we know the real agony they will undergo in the days ahead.

MISS LYONS LEAVES THE D. C. SCHOOLS
After 50 Years a New Beginning

BY CORNELIA BALL

A woman who has spent practically all her life in the District school system is retiring the end of this month, and tonight her friends are honoring her at a reception.

Miss Edith A. Lyons, a teacher, principal and administrator for 50 years, reached the mandatory retirement age of 70 earlier in the year. More than 2000 persons have bought tickets for tonight's party at the Sheraton-Park to tell her good-bye.

MOVED

Miss Lyons, a slender woman with a fondness for pretty hats, was born in Augusta, Ga. But her parents moved to the District in time for her to be educated in Washington's public schools.

She went to Garrison, and the old M-st school, and was graduated from the old Miner Normal School (now part of D.C. Teachers College) in 1914. She started teaching the first grade at Stevens School the following January, when she was 20.

She went right up the line—teaching fourth grade, then sixth, and in 1928, Miss Lyons was named assistant to the director of primary instruction. In 1930 she became administrative principal of the Morgan Demonstration School.

She still lives not far from there—at 1833 S-st nw. That was handy in those day, she said, because Morgan was a seven-day-a-week job.

KIND WORDS

The School Board, in a tribute to her at its April meeting, said that "in the community of the Morgan School, Miss Lyons was principal, teacher, mother and benefactor, and on many occasions, family consultant. She loved her work, and in her usual competent and efficient manner, did a superior job."

But in 1942 she was called back to school headquarters as supervising principal of Division 13, and in 1950 was made Director of Elementary Education in charge of Supervision for colored children.

When the public schools desegregated here in 1954, Miss Lyons was named assistant superintendent of the combined elementary schools, the first Negro to reach that high a post in the local system.

"When the history of the

MISS EDITH LYONS

desegregation of the public schools of the District of Columbia is finally recorded ... the name of Edith A. Lyons should be written on top of the honor roll for the major contributions she has made to the honor roll for the major contributions she has made to the successful welding of the two divisions of the elementary department ... This has not been an easy task," the School Board tribute said.

Retirement isn't going to find Miss Lyons idle.

"There are a lot of things I hope to do. I'll always volunteer my services to the Congress of Parents and Teachers. Any P-TA that needs me just has to call ...

"I can't get away from little children. After I take a breather I'm going to volunteer my services to Headstart. Just anything they want me to do.

"I want to do some work for my church — that's St. Luke's Episcopal — and I'm interested in politics. I'm a really good Democrat. And I want to travel.

"I've had a wonderful life with the school system. I've enjoyed every single day. I'll miss it terribly—all the fine people, the teachers, the parents, the children and our wonderful superintendent. My years here have been golden years."

Tributes to Members of the Washington, D.C. Public School System and Dawson, Georgia

To: Miss Edith A. Lyons
On the Occasion of Her Retirement as Assistant Superintendent of Elementary Schools in the District of Columbia, June 2, 1965*

Elegant Lady of the District of Columbia Schools,
    you have performed your
Duties diligently, and with equanimity
    disciplined the
Ideas that your creative mind brought forth.
    You have exemplified
Tolerance towards others as well as displaying
Humility in your every deed.

Attaining one success after another,
    you have engendered affection through a dedicated

Life of helping others and giving many
Years of service to humanity.
    Inspiring along the way,
Originality of thought, and embracing with open arms,
    value born of the mind and soul, the essence of
Noble dreams envisioned the realities of today;
    this memorable profile of
Selflessness, your gift to all—peers, colleagues,
    parents, and children.

*Presented to Miss Lyons for her scrapbook, June 2, 1965, Washington, D.C.

A

RECEPTION

honoring

MISS EDITH A. LYONS

On the occasion of her retirement

from

THE PUBLIC SCHOOLS

of the

DISTRICT OF COLUMBIA

SHERATON PARK HOTEL
Grand Ballroom
Wednesday, June 2, 1965
Six to eight p.m.

PROGRAM

Greetings   Mr. John M. Riecks
Deputy Superintendent of Schools

Music   H. D. Cooke School Choral Group

TO HONOR MISS EDITH A. LYONS

                   Honorable Walter N. Tobriner, President
Board of Commissioners
District of Columbia

A SALUTE FROM THE CITIZENS

                   Honorable John B. Duncan
Commissioner
District of Columbia

A SALUTE FROM THE MUNICIPAL DEPARTMENTS

                   Honorable Wesley S. Williams
President
Board of Education

A SALUTE FROM THE BOARD OF EDUCATION

                   Honorable Carl F. Hansen
Superintendent of Schools
District of Columbia

A SALUTE FROM THE PUBLIC SCHOOLS

Music   H. D. Cooke School Choral Group

Presentation of Gifts

Acceptance   Miss Edith A. Lyons
Assistant Superintendent of Schools

Music   H. D. Cooke School Choral Group

To Mrs. Theresa C. Alexander
Supervising Director of the Division of Guidance Services
Public School System, Washington, D.C., June, 1967

    The true test of your success required
    Hard work, harmonious relationships, and the
    Enjoyment of every task that you performed.
    Rapport was gained through
    Exchange of ideas,
    Service above reproach, and
    Acceptance of the premise that each individual
        is unique unto himself.

    Counselors and Guidance Workers everywhere,

    Appreciate the gift you have bequested:
    Love of Life,
    Energy to perform our daily tasks, and an
    X-ray technique for developing our skills.
    Always remember you still have
    Numerous challenges to
    Design for the good of all Guidance Workers; and we
    Envision a future of happiness for you as a
    Reward for laying a solid foundation upon which
        we may continue to build.

To Mrs. Lillie M. Cooper
On the Occasion of
"The Lillie Cooper P.T.A. Presents a Tribute to . . ."
Dawson, Georgia, May 19, 1968

ELEGANT
Lady of the Terrell County, Georgia
   Public School System:
YOU HAVE:
Inspired youth in their search for selfhood.
Lauded and supported the idea of an education for all.
Lived a life dedicated to humanity.
Instilled in each individual a desire to succeed, and
Encouraged everyone who needed your support.

Meliorism played an important role in your endeavor to
   better understand mankind.

YOU DID BEQUEATH:
Confidence in one's self,
Open-minded views on world problems,
Observance of educational goals,
Perseverance at all times,
Enthusiasm for each daily task, and
Refinement in its highest degree.

LILLIE COOPER P. T. A.

- Presents A Tribute To -

Mrs. Lillie M. Cooper

Lillie Cooper Elementary School
May 19, 1968 -:- 6:00 - 7:00 P. M.

MRS. MARY R. MILNER, President — MR. J. T. GORDON, Principal

Guests of Honor

ALL RETIRED TEACHERS

— AND —

P. T. A. OFFICERS OF ALL SCHOOLS

Ushers

Mrs. Arris Hamilton	Lillie Cooper
Mrs. Catherine Young	Dunbar Elementary
Mrs. Carrie E. Glover	Carver Elementary
Mrs. Daisy K. Daniels	Martin Elementary
Miss L. P. Chester	Helen Gurr Elementary
Mrs. L. M. Benjamin	Carver High School

Program Committee

Mrs. M. R. Milner	Chairman
Mrs. L. M. Benjamin	Secretary

Mrs. V. C. Floyd	Mrs. F. Wakefield
Mrs. J. R. Lewis	Mrs. M. D. Beasley
Mrs. M. L. Carter	Mrs. C. B. Humphries

PROGRAM

* * * * * * *

MAY 19, 1968 — 6:00 - 7:00 P. M.

* * * * * * *

Song — "Lift Every Voice And Sing"	Audience
Scripture	Mrs. Jessie Marshall
Prayer	Dr. E. E. Sykes
Song — "O God, Our Help In Ages Past"	Audience
Greeting	Mr. J. T. Gordon
Choral Selection	Lillie Cooper Chorus
Tributary	Mrs. Ceola Jeffers
Selection	Carver High School Chorus
Introduction of Speaker	Mrs. Janie Lewis
Address	Mr. R. R. Aaron
	President, Terrell County Teachers Association
Choral Selection	Dunbar Chorus
Response	Mrs. S. S. Moore
	Curriculum Director
Teachers' Creed	Terrell County Teachers Ensemble
Presentation of Flowers	Mrs. M. R. Milner
	President, Lillie Cooper P. T. A.
Unveiling of Portrait	Mr. C. Williams
Announcements	Mr. J. T. Gordon
Dismissal	Rev. B. M. Motley

"O GOD, OUR HELP IN AGES PAST"

* * * * * * *

O God, our help in a-ges past,
Our hope for years to come,
Our shel-ter from the storm-y blast,
And our e-ter-nal Home!

Be-fore the hills in or-der stood,
Or earth re-ceived her frame,
From ev-er-lasting Thou art God,
To end-less years the same.

To Mrs. Mildred U. Alfred
On the Occasion of Her Retirement
(Teacher at the Charles Young School, Washington, D.C.)

Majestic Lady of the District of Columbia
    Public School System: You Have
Inspired youth to attain selfhood;
Lauded and supported the idea of an education for all;
Devoted your life to serving mankind;
Respected the rights of others;
Encouraged everyone who sought advice;
    and, performed with
Deftness many duties.

Through an

Understanding of human needs, you instilled in each
    individual a desire to achieve.

Aspiration,
Loyalty,
Friendship,
Refinement,
Enthusiasm, and
Dedication are the attributes that you contributed
    to the teaching profession.

To Mrs. Mabel S. Hatcher
On the Occasion of Her Retirement
(Teacher, Charles Young School)

Majestic Lady of the District of Columbia
    Public School System: Your—
Acceptance of individual differences,
Belief in humanity,
Enthusiasm for education, and through
Leadership, many youth became well-rounded.

Sincerity played an important role in
    character building for all youth.

Honesty,
Appreciation,
Tolerance,
Confidence,
Hope,
Efficiency, and
Refinement are the attributes that you
    instilled in each individual.

To Mrs. Julia Young Fickling
*On the Occasion of Her Retirement
(Supervising Director of the
Division of Guidance Service, Washington, D.C.)
November 30, 1970*

We are Congratulating you for setting the *stage* upon which Elementary School Counselors could *perform*.

Thank you for the many hours of "sweat and toil" that produced the *scene*. Through the courses that you taught: Guidance, Counseling Techniques, and Practicum, we received our *dialogue*. At *rehearsals* (Weekly Workshops), we were *directed* to serve humanity. In the schools we mastered our skills and interpreted our *lines*. As the *curtain* closed on our first *presentation*, the *audience* gave us a *standing ovation*.

We all wish you happiness, good health, and a relaxing holiday from the everyday grind.

May God Bless You and Your Family!

Marguerite Mitchell Marshall
Counselor at the Charles Young School
Washington, D.C. 1970

RETIREMENT PARTY FOR GUIDANCE DIRECTOR

By MABS KEMP, Social Columnist,
Afro American Newspaper

Mrs. Julia Y. Fickling was the guest of honor Saturday at a luncheon on the occasion of her retirement as Supervising Director in the Guidance Division of the Public Schools of the District of Columbia.

The affair brought together almost 400 of the honoree's friends and co-workers; and began with a noon reception at which guests toasted Mrs. Fickling and her family and wished her godspeed, happiness and good luck at this point in her life.

Receiving with Mrs. Fickling at the reception were her husband, Judge Austin L. Fickling; her daughter and son-in-law, Mr. and Mrs. Criss Glaude, Mrs. Muriel Alexander, a member of the Board of Education and Henrietta B. Franklin of the Roosevelt High School faculty and chairman of the luncheon.

At exactly one o'clock, guests retired to the Cotillion Room where lunch was served. The decor of the lavish dining room was in keeping with the favorite flower and colors of the honoree--red and pink and the carnation.

RETIREMENT PARTY FOR GUIDANCE DIRECTOR - Continued

Immediately following lunch, which was preceded by the welcome remarks of Mrs. Franklin and grace by Miss Annie P. Barden, was a timely program of music, tributes and introductions. Mrs. B. K. Williams, luncheon co-chairman, very cleverly introduced members of the honoree's family and special luncheon guests; while Mrs. Felicia E. Glascoe, another co-chairman, gave the main tribute to Mrs. Fickling. Mrs. Barbara B. White, soprano, sang "An Affair to Remember," and "Love Is A Many Splendored Thing." She was accompanied at the piano by Miss Cozette Carter.

Interspersed between the musical numbers were "many, mini" greetings. They included Norman W. Nickens, School Administration; Muriel M. Alexander, Board of Education; Gary Freeman, Pupil Personnel Services; Lucille Gayle, Guidance Division; Aileen H. Davis, a former colleague; Marion C. Shapiro, Counselor; John D. Koontz, Associate Superintendent; Sojourner E. Jackson, Assistant Principal; Milton Denbo, Mental Health Association; Paulette M. Morgan, Project O.P.E.N.; Jane Baldwin, Telephone Company; Katherine Cole, American Personnel and Guidance Association; H. R. Crawford, a former counselee; Annie P. Barden, Counselor and Paul Collins, D.C. School Counselor Association. Dr. Alfred E. Simons, Jr., furnished luncheon music.

Highlight of the afternoon was the presentation by Mrs. Franklin of a $1,000 Bond - all done up and attached prettily to a miniature 747 airliner - described as the preliminary step to a life of relaxation and travel. There were long-stemmed roses, wires and other gifts.

Mrs. Fickling, in response to the many tributes, expressed thanks - saying that the gesture had been the most emotional and heart-warming experience of her life. It was "... truly an affair to remember," she stated. She had nothing but accolades for her counselors and the persons she had counseled. Mrs. Marion R. Flagg put the final touch to the program with a poem written in Mrs. Fickling's honor.

The committee responsible for the luncheon were: Paul F. Bush, Emma M. Carter, Marion R. Flagg, Lucille J. Gayle, Mary J. Gross, Nathaniel E. Hill, Calvin H. Holt, Frankie V. Houchins, Sojourner E. Jackson, William G. Liggins, Lovella S Lowe, Vivian I. Montague, Sara A. Moultrie, Melvin C. Riddick, Marion C. Shapiro, Lillie J. VanLandingham, Henrietta B. Franklin, Felicia E. Glascoe and Blanche K. Williams.

To: Mrs. Idella M. Costner
On the Occasion of her Retirement—July 31, 1977
(Teacher, Charles Young Elementary School, Washington, D.C.)

        With an
Incentive to work for improving humanity, you persisted in
Dedication to your duty.
        Striving daily for
Excellence and endurance provided a better understanding of
    life for your students.
Loyalty, and
Love of home, school, and community stimulated their
Aspiration to achieve.

Modesty is the key that opened the door to your success.

Consideration for others,
Obedience to God's Will,
Self-sacrifice.
Tolerance, and
Natural instinct added
Enlightenment to your
Responsibility to mankind.

To: Mrs. Piccola H. Dukes
On the Occasion of her Retirement—July 31, 1977
(Teacher, Charles Young Elementary School, Washington, D.C.)

Gifted with
Proficiency, you did set standards and
Ideals for your students to attain.
Courage gave them a different point of view.
Cooperation and fulfilling one's
Obligations to society engendered growth.
A broader outlook on
Life enhanced each student's
Ability to survive in the world.

Humility is the basis of your success.

Devotion to duty,
Understanding the needs of humans.
Knowledge of life, and
Efficiency gave
Stability to your career.

Poems

Prairie Wildlife in the Fall

The Prairie is all aglow in the Fall . . . brown sedge and rush swaying with the gentle breeze; the orange-red-brown leaves falling softly from the trees; and, the crimson sumac vines clinging tenaciously to a tree.

As quick as a flash, the jack rabbit leaps across the dirt road.
He is followed by the prairie dog, the woodchuck, the squirrel, and the ferret.
Each left his habitat to seek shelter and safety from the huntsmen.

The ping of the Rifle,
The bark of the Irish Setter,
The flapping of the wings of birds, as they leave the bushes and trees, are sounds that their keen, sharp senses of hearing, smelling, and seeing perceive as signals that hunters are nearby.

The Plains no longer remain serene and silent.
Once, only the happy, quiet sounds of birds and animals could be heard.
Now man begins his yearly trek over the land, and upsets the balance of nature.

Alas, the animals and the birds know that they must survive.
They know the destructive forces that disturb their lives.
Therefore, they move to other places that offer the protection they need.

Prairie Wildlife in the Winter

Winter is a cold, hard and bitter season for wildlife on the Prairie.
The eight or ten inches of snow that blankets the earth eliminates the sounds of birds and animals.
It is very quiet and still now.
There is seldom a sign of life astir.

After the snow melts, a few birds and animals may venture out in search of sustenance.
But many remain pacifiably in their dormancy.

"Where are these creatures of Nature?" I ask.
The answer comes back: Some are in warmer climates, some are buried beneath the earth, while still others may have remained here.

So you toss out bird seeds and bits of food to feed the ones who are around,
Hoping that Spring will offer an incentive for them to return.

Prairie Wildlife in the Spring

    Early in the morning,
We hear the musical mating calls of the blackbirds, bluejays, bobolinks, cowbirds, meadowlarks, robins, and sparrows.
We see the robins, bluejays, and meadowlarks diligently building homes for their young.

    With the sun shining brightly,
  and the temperature 70 degrees,
A mother skunk and her brood venture out in search of food.
The salt-pepper gray badger, with the white stripe from its nose down its back, busily digging out a ground squirrel.
A family of four young prairie dogs sitting on a mound watching and waiting for a chance to give life outside a whirl.
A gray gopher, with a birdlike whistle, calling to his mate.
The box turtle slowly trudging to an old burrow.
The brood of six ground squirrels already showing signs of 'independence before estivation.

    With the sun slowly sinking
in the West,
We feel the peace and solitude that only the prairies offer.

    At night,
We hear the:
    ki-yipping howl of coyotes,
    chirping of crickets,
    whee-ool sound of a long-legged owl,
    kill-kill-kill shrill call of the killdeer.

    All of these sights, sounds, and movements attest to the fact that Spring has arrived, and wildlife is now at its best.

Prairie Wildlife in the Summer

Some sights to see:

Flowers — abloom over the vast plains—forbs with hues of yellow, blue, pink, brown, and white, the blazing star, cone flowers, purple prairie clover, wild indigo, and brown-eyed Susan.

Grasses — that are 4–5 feet tall—midgrasses (Western wheat grass with blue-green stands), Prairie sage, Range grass, and the June grass.

Shrubs — less than 12 feet tall: Buffalo berry—silver in color Wolfberry—often called snowberry Silveryberry—white, hoary leaves.

Butterflies — floating gracefully through the air: Monarch, Buckeye, and Viceroy with their black bordered, orange-brown wings.

Some sounds to hear:

Grasshoppers — flitting from plant to plant: Longhorn and Shorthorn, making a chirr-chirr sound.

Birds	chirping and chirping as they pluck worms from the warm, moist earth—Redbirds, Robins, Bluejays, and Meadowlarks.
Prairie Chickens	as they perform their mating ritual of dance and strut.
Animals	such as the Cottontails that brush noisily through the thicket and shrubs. The Prairie Wolf with the coyote yelp.

Some things to feel:

Early-morning drops a dew on the plants,
The wind's gentle breeze in your face,
The sun brightly shining through a window pane as the morn turns to day.
The rain, falling softly upon the earth to breathe new life into the arid sod.

This is the life that survives on the Prairies in the summer.

Autumn in Kansas

Autumn is a favorite season for all Kansans. The reasons follow:

1. The wonderful Indian summer weather stimulates both body and soul.
2. We are the recipients of a bountiful harvest of crops, grains, and fruits.
3. We have the unique privilege of attending and participating in county and state fairs.

The Indian summer weather is superb. Our daily temperatures range from 56–75 degrees; and the wind from the southwest swirls across the prairie like a giant tumbleweed. An intermittent thunderstorm does not upset the balance of nature—it settles the dust, moistens the farmlands, and brings relief to those working in the fields.

It is harvest time, and the farmer is busy preparing his crops, grains, and fruits for the market and for home use. The 4H and FFA groups are engaged in grooming and fattening up the hogs, cattle, steers, and poultry for market and to enter contests at the fairs. Other groups are sewing and making handicrafts for this event. The women will be occupied with the canning of vegetables, drying fruits, making pickles, jams, and jellies for the fair and family consumption. They also help process the meat.

Apple butter making in Mound City, Kansas, and Mt. Vernon, Missouri, is another special occasion in autumn. Large, wrought-iron kettles are filled with pared and cored apples with a fire beneath the kettle—prepared on Main Street—where everyone can participate. When the apples boil and bubble, sugar and spices are added and stirred frequently. Samples are placed in a bowl on tables nearby with other foods, and anyone can eat as much as they wish before the ladies ladle the remaining apple butter into jars.

Autumn splendor (photo for the Pittsburg, Kansas *Morning Sun* by Kevin Vivers)

The Black Walnut Harvest is another special event. The walnuts are knocked from the trees, loaded into baskets, and sent to the factory for shelling. The uses for the walnut include: paint, seal, dental industry for filling, jet motors, and for cooking cakes, cookies, and candy.

The culmination of all of these activities takes place at the county or state fairs. Here we enjoy the big rodeo, fiddlers' contest, musical, theatrical, and talent shows. The second day there is the cattle, hogs, steer, and poultry-judging contests. The women participate in baking, canning, jelly, jams, pickles, and piccalilli contests. Many booths contain handicrafts and hobbies that capture one's fancy. As the fair ends, the rides are disassembled, booths closed and everyone is homeward bound with ribbons, cash, and a happy heart. All of the above vigorous actions in autumn enliven life for the people who live and work in Kansas.

Kansas snow scene

Sek Mountains—peaks of strip mine refuse between Arma and Girard, Kansas (Pittsburg, Kansas *Morning Sun* photo)

A Sonnet to the Snow

The snow quietly covered the earth last night.
Now, like a graceful white swan, it will stretch
Across the Prairie, soft and feather light.
Caressed by the sunlight, we see it etch
A picture fusing of earth, sun, and snow.
There is a crisp, cold, chill-feel in the air
That can tingle one's spirit to a glow.
We feel spellbound by your splendor so rare.
Children may indulge in a snowball game:
Some may enjoy a long, brisk walk alone.
Others sit, observe, and admire how tame
You make everything with your soft tone.

Ah, Snow! Your benefits we oft reason,
Yet Nature crowns you "King of the Seasons."

"Snow Devil"—a statue covered with ice at the Cranbrook Academy of Art in Bloomfield Hills

The Winter of 1976-1977

Our first snowfall, in Kansas, on December 28, 1976, was very light—only 4 inches.

January 2, 1977. Eighteen to Twenty-four inches of snow covered many areas of the region. Streets and highways became impassable. The next two days of rain and sleet added to our plight.

More snow followed until we had a total of Ten Snow Days in January, and Thirty-one Days of Freezing Temperatures—ranging from (-15 degrees) to 10 degrees with no relief in sight.

On January 10, 1977, Buffalo, New York was a blanket of snow with ten feet covering the earth for three weeks.

Nome, Alaska had a mild winter.

Other cities receiving eight feet or less included:
    Charleston, West Virginia—"Snow Roller"
    Chicago, Illinois—12 inches
    Dayton, Ohio—14 inches
    Detroit, Michigan—4 feet
    Louisville, Kentucky—2 feet
    Minneapolis, Minnesota—6 feet
    New York City—Rain and 10 inches of snow.

Orlando, Orange County, Florida sustained severe damage to the fruit and vegetable crops. With the freezing temperatures and frost killing the crops, they lost millions of dollars.

The cause, according to the Weather Bureau: "Shift in Wind Patterns"—gusts to 40 miles—cold Arctic air from the North, Canada, and Greenland.

With this ice, snow and sub-zero temperatures, we were dealt another exceptional occurrence—A Heating Problem arose—gas and oil shortage—because the zero and subzero temperatures had drained the natural gas reserves to critical levels.

The Government stated that "We must:
   (1) turn our thermostats to 65 degrees;
   (2) close doors of rooms in our homes and offices not being used;
   (3) wear warm clothing; and
   (4) do not go outside unless very urgent."

School doors closed, office workers and government employees were off. Industries shut down, and many workers were released as a result of the power shortage—machinery and equipment could not operate. Travelers Advisories were in effect. All social activities and sports events were curtailed to conserve fuel. Deaths due to exposure were prevalent. Many people sustained "Frost Bites," from overexposure. Others endured broken bones as a result of a fall on the ice or slippery porches.

The Winter of 1976–1977 will be recorded as a complex phenomenon that was unforeseen.

A Sonnet to Christ, the Cross Bearer

I see Christ as He trudges up the hill
Looking so sorrow-laden and forlorn;
Carrying the heavy wooden Cross until,
Bent beneath its weight, He feels all worn.
He pauses briefly to regain control
Of the burden only to fall again.
Simon of Cyrene lifts the Cross so bold,
On to Golgotha, a trial to sustain.
Arriving at "the place of a skull," now
They crucify Him and part his garments
Casting lots on what each should take, and how.
Not a word of woe, not a soft lament.

The Saviour died for our sins, we learn
And we never gave Him love in return.

Drawing of Christ carrying the cross

The Resurrection

Joseph of Arimathea removed our Saviour from the Cross.
He wrapped the body in a linen cloth, gently and with feal,
Laid it in a tomb. What a loss!
A stone was rolled up to the entrance of the sepulcher
    as a seal.

On the third day, Christ arose to effect
A mighty triumph o'er the grave.
We sing Hallelujah for a victory so select
Knowing that now we have eternal life with Him
    —this He gave.

"Peace be unto you," spake He to the disciples, and showed
    them his hands, feet and side.
The disciples were glad to see the Lord.
After eight days with them, He blessed them and was carried
    up into Heaven.

HOSANNA IN THE HIGHEST!

Essays

Christmas in My Hometown (Pittsburg, Kansas) 1920

After World War I, our veterans returned home, and during the 1920s, families began to put more sparkle into their daily lives. The men whistled, and the women hummed various tunes on their way to and from work. Everyone was happy to be home, to be with his family, and returning to the task of earning a living.

The Saturday following Thanksgiving Day was reserved for the children's annual visit with Santa Claus at Ramsay's Department Store—517 North Broadway. This was an event that we looked forward to for several reasons. First: a line was formed outside the store, and with Santa Claus leading, we walked on the West Side of Broadway to Fourth Street and back on the East Side of Broadway to Ramsay's. Second: inside the store, each child was presented, by Santa Claus, an old-fashioned 12-inch, round, peppermint stick of candy wrapped in cellophane. Everyone enjoyed talking with Santa, shaking his hand, and hearing the big "Ho-Ho-Ho" laugh that he made. The younger children were frightened, at first, by reason of his red-white suit and long, white beard. However, they never refused the candy. Each year, we were presented a different treat—sometimes a bag of candy and nuts, and other times candy and fruit, but my favorite was the long peppermint stick because it lasted longer.

Years later, we were informed by friends that Santa Claus was played by our father, Henry Levi Mitchell. My brother and I were very hurt and disappointed because we assumed that Santa Claus was real. Mother asked us to keep the secret since the two younger sisters believed in Santa; and she urged us to continue to go and enjoy it for their sake. The Santa Claus event was started in 1920 under the supervision of the manager, Mr. J. W. Overby, and terminated in 1933.

Store windows were decorated with toys, gift ideas, and Christmas trees trimmed with tinsel, large, red socks filled with small toys, and ornamental balls. The hardware stores featuring toys included: Ridgway, Beasley and Miller, Sell and Sons, and Deruy's. S. H. Kress and Woolworth also carried toys. The department stores—Frolich, Fleishaker, Coulter-McGuire, Drunagel, Globe Clothing, Holden-Ward, Newman, Ramsay's, and Seymour's—all displayed adult and children's gift ideas.

Schools and churches occupied the children's time with plays and programs. Adult activities included shopping, cleaning the house, and cooking. One week prior to Christmas, most homes had purchased and decorated a Christmas tree. When gifts arrived from relatives, friends, and neighbors, they were placed under the tree. Toys, removed from their secret hiding places, did not come out until midnight on Christmas eve. On Christmas morning, elation, excitement, and joy filled the children's hearts; and as our parents watched, a twinkle would be noted in their eyes.

Mrs. Carrie Jameison tells us that "the Christmas spirit begins Friday after Thanksgiving Day when the decorations on Broadway have been completed. The shopping, preparation for church programs, parties, and the excitement of little children around the Christmas tree with all the family together are still vivid to me."

Mrs. Darlene Mitchell states: "The city's overhead decorations swinging from each lamp pole and lighted after five o'clock; children talking to Santa Claus and having a photograph made with him; the friendly atmosphere of the shoppers and clerks; and my father-in-law and husband decorating our homes, along with my mother coming over to cook

Christmas goodies; the Sunday school programs, all of these are among my most enjoyable memories in Pittsburg."

Mrs. Archieleen Greene looks forward to the Christmas season in Pittsburg for two reasons: "We have the most beautiful Christmas lights that hang along Broadway that I have ever seen; and the Carver League Programs for the children and adults help to bring forth the Christmas spirit."

Mrs. Earline Davis believes that "large cities cannot compete with Pittsburg as far as the beautiful, overhead lights and decorations are concerned. To drive or walk on Broadway at Christmas makes one feel joyful."

Mrs. Oma Hawkins remembers many activities that occurred prior to Christmas. "On Christmas eve, the family popped corn to be strung together with thread and placed on the tree along with the lights. We prepared cranberries and different vegetables so that we would not have too much to do on Christmas. After the gifts had been placed around the tree, we would listen to Christmas carols on the radio until bedtime."

As one visualizes the various activities described above, one may conclude that "Christmas is a family tradition, passed on from generation to generation, in My Hometown of Pittsburg, Kansas."

The First Celebration
of the Pittsburg Homecoming Club
July 6-8, 1962

On July 6, 1962, registration and a program were the opening events. A picnic followed on July 7, 1962. Sunday church services were held at the Mt. Hebron Baptist Church with Rev. Elmer Newton, pastor of Trinity Methodist Church, Kansas City, Missouri, in charge. Solos were performed by Mr. Carl A. Cain from France, and Mr. Colen Scales from Des Moines, Iowa. The queen, crowned at the July 6 event, was Ms. Judy Turner, Pittsburg, Kansas.

Officers:

Mr. Miles J. Cole, *president*
Mr. William Pierce, *vice-president*
Mrs. Catherine Berger, *secretary*
Mrs. Deloris Rogers, *assistant secretary*
Mrs. Ethel McGee, *financial secretary*
Mrs. Allie Kelly, *treasurer*
Mrs. Neva C. Beatty, *program chairman*
Mrs. Glyncora Wilburn, *general chairman*

PROGRAM

Friday July 6, 1962

Reception ---------------------- Eight to Ten P. M.

LINCOLN PARK AUDITORIUM

Glyncora Wilburn ------------------ Chairman

Sat. July 7, 1962

Social Period

Time - 2:00 P. M.

FREE REFRESHMENTS

GAMES FOR YOUTH

Mr. Theodore Allmon - Mr. Lloyd Cole Beatty, Jr.
Mr. Wm. J. Pierce ------------------- Chairman

Dance Sat. Nite 9 till 1 P. M.

TOWER BALLROOM

NORTH BDWY.

Sponsored by the AMERICAN LEGION OF PITTSBURG

SUNDAY JULY 8, 1962
Mt. Hebron Bapt. Church
310 East 10th Street
S. M. Stevenson - Pastor
Morning Worship 10:45 A. M.

Devotionals -- Mrs. Allie Kelly - Mr. C. Dial, Sr.
Processional ------------------------------- Choir
Call to Worship
Welcome ------------------ Mrs. Herbert Wilson
Response ---- Mrs. Andrew Funkhouser, Joplin, Mo.
Solo
Scripture ------------------------------- Pastor
Solo ------------------------ Mrs. E. B. Martin
Announcements
Solo ---------------------------- Mr. Carl Cain
Meditation ---------------------------- Pastor
Introduction of Speaker ----- Mr. C.E. Walker
Sermon ---------- Rev. E.W. Newton, K.C. Kansas
Invitation ------------------------------ Pastor
Offertory
Remarks ----------------------- Neva Beatty

BENEDICTION

Program Committee ---------- Mrs. Mattye Foxx
                            Mrs. Catherine Berger

Dinner Will Be Served at Lincoln Park at 1:30 P.M.

On the Second Anniversary of the Pittsburg Homecoming Club
July 9–11, 1965

PITTSBURGERS

Pleasant are the memories that we will share, at this
Inspiring and historic event; designed
To be recorded as a reminder of our living and growing up here, and
To be cherished by everyone forever.
Satisfying will be the occasion when we
Bestow upon loved ones and friends timely greetings, and
Utter praises of our hometown.
Realizing the importance of returning to our native land, makes us
Grateful for the opportunity to
Embrace the idea of
Reliving once more the days of yore.
Sweet are the sounds that echo welcome to the Second Anniversary of the Pittsburg Homecoming Club.

Officers

Mr. Miles Cole, *President*
Mr. William Pierce, *Vice-President*
Mrs. Catherine Berger, *Secretary*
Mrs. Deloris Rogers, *Assistant Secretary*
Mrs. Allie Kelly, *Treasurer*
Mrs. Glyncora Wilburn, *General Chairman*
Mrs. Ethel McGee, *Financial Secretary*

Queen

Mrs. Mary Williams

Reception and Queen Contest
Friday, July 9, 1965

Mrs. Ethel Cole ------------------------------------Chairman
Mrs. Melvin Woods---------------------Mistress of Ceremony
Mrs. Robert Carson--------------------------------------Pianist

Prelude of Music---------------------Negro National Anthem
Invocation--------------------------------Rev. Leroy Nelson
Welcome------------------------------------Mr. William Pierce
Solo--Mrs. Melvin Wood
Greetings--------------------------Mayor O. Gene Bicknell
Duet--------------------------------Miss Nette & Bette Sharp
Response---------------------------------Mr. Robert Caldwell
Solo------------------------------------- Mrs. Melvin Wood
Reading------------------------------ Miss Barbara Stephens

Music Interlude
"Queen Parade"

Mrs. Helen Pierce----------------------------Topeka, Kansas
Mrs. Florence Martin -----------------------Hannibal, Mo.
Mrs. Mary Williams-----------------------Pittsburg, Kansas
Mrs. Edith Martin--------------------------Kansas City, Mo.

Introduction of Officers

Mr. Miles Cole------------------------------------President
Mr. Billie Pierce---------------------------Vice-President
Mrs. Catherine Berger ----------------------------Secretary
Mrs. Deloris Rogers-----------------------Ass't. Secretary
Mrs. Ethel McGee-----------------------Financial Secretary
Mrs. Allie Kelly-----------------------------------Treasure
Mrs. Glyncora Wilburn -------------- Gen. Program Chairman

Introduction of Kansas City Club

Remarks:--------------------------President, Mr. Miles Cole
Committee Members
Chairman--------------------------------------Mrs. Ethel Cole
Co-Chairman--------------------------------Mrs. Mammie Martin
Secy. Treasurer----------------------------Mrs. Marie Toney
Mrs. Mattye Foxx   Mrs. Frances Danforth
Mrs. Ethel McGee   Mrs. Glyncora Wilburn

On the Third Anniversary of the Pittsburg Homecoming Club
July 7–9, 1972

"IN RETROSPECT"*

We have assembled for the third time to give meaning to the fact that as a Kansan first and as a Pittsburger second, our purpose is to continue to make this a historical event that will be written in the annals for many decades.

As loyal and law-abiding citizens, third, it is hoped that recognition of our actions will become so noteworthy that everyone here will participate.

To our friends, who came from far and near, we give a hearty welcome and pray that Our Heavenly Father will bless you always. Upon returning to your homes, we trust that you will strive to keep this affair functioning.

To the president, committees, and members who worked so diligently, we extend our thanks and best wishes. To my sponsor, Miss Elvira Williams, "Many thanks for a job well done."

Officers

Mrs. Catherine Berger, *President*
Mr. Charles Dial, Sr. *Vice-President*
Mrs. Juanita Gilmore, *Secretary*
Mr. Lloyd Beatty, *Asst. Secretary*
Mr. Hugh Green, *Financial Secretary*
Mr. Edward Gilmore, *Treasurer*
Mrs. Glyncora Wilburn, *General Program Chairman*

---

*Speech prepared by the writer on the occasion of being crowned Pittsburg Homecoming Club Queen, July 7, 1972.

PROGRAM

Friday   LINCOLN CENTER   July 7, 1972

Registration ... 6:30-8:00 P.M.
Negro National Anthem
Invocation ... Elder Walter Dorsey, Sr.
Welcome ... Mrs. Catherine Berger
Response ... Mr. George Dismuke
Instrumental Duet ... Masters Melvin & Martin Foxx
Greetings ... Mayor, Curtiss Nettles
Solo ... Mrs. Barbara Lee
Introduction of Speaker ... S.Sgt. Reba Litman
Speaker ... Dr. Hazle Blakeney
Solo ... Mrs. Barbara Lee

MUSICAL INTERLUDE

Queen Coronation ... Miss Judy Turner, Kansas City, Missouri

Contestants   Sponsors

Mrs. Ozella Craig   Mrs. Neva Beatty
Topeka, Kansas

Mrs. Allena Funkhouser   Mrs. Catherine Berger
Joplin, Missouri

Mrs. Verna Kerr   Mr. Hugh Green
Wichita, Kansas

Mrs. Marguerite Marshall   Miss Elvira Williams
Washington, D.C.

INTRODUCTION OF OFFICERS

"THE BOND" PRESENTATION

RECEPTION

Sunday   July 9, 1972

Morning Worship Service Lincoln Center
11:00 A.M.

Devotionals: Mrs. Allie Kelly, Mrs. Mable Chipley
Mr. Johnny Pierce, Mr. Charles Dial

Congregational Song ... Pass Me Not
Welcome ... Mrs. Audrey Scroggins
Response ... Mayor, Robert Caldwell
Solo ... Mr. Paul Melvin Burnett
Scripture ... Elder Elzie Allmon
Prayer ... Rev. Henry Pullum
Congregational Song ... Yield Not To Temptation
Offertory ... Charles Whitcomb, Jr. & Mr. Lloyd Beatty
Offertory Prayer ... Rev Louis Glenn

Soft Music

Solo ... Mr. Donald Smith
Memoriam ... Mrs. Florence Martin
Solo ... Mr. Paul Melvin Burnett
Introduction of Speaker ... Rev. S.M. Stevenson
Speaker ... Chaplain Melvin Woods
Invitation ... Rev. S.M. Stevenson
Solo ... Mr. Paul Melvin Burnett
Remarks ... Mrs. Catherine Berger
Benediction ... Rev. Lorenzo R. Finnell

Pianist ... Mrs. Mattye Foxx
Accompaniment ... Mrs. Caldonia Smith

Dinner will be served in the Lincoln Park Shelter House #1 at 12:30 P.M. Please present your Meal Ticket.

On the Fourth Anniversary
of the Pittsburg Homecoming Club
July 11–13, 1975

Again we assemble—for this historic event—to celebrate the fourth anniversary of the Pittsburg Homecoming Club.

Mrs. Catherine T. Berger, president, opened the program, at Lincoln Center on July 11, 1975, with a welcome. Mr. Laurence Glenn from Detroit, Michigan, gave the Response. Our reception chairperson, Mrs. Darlene Mitchell, introduced the mayor of the city, Mrs. Ruth Lemon.

Two former classmates held us spellbound on the program: Mr.Thurston Graham, acting chief administrator, Social Security Administration, Baltimore, Maryland, introduced the speaker. Mrs. Genevieve M. Shedrick, teacher in Dawson, Georgia, spoke on the subject "Freedom, Our Greatest Task, Will Lead to Growth and Wealth of Progress."

The coronation of the king, Mr. Milton Glenn, Los Angeles, California, and the queen, Mrs. Donna M. Freeman, Kansas City, Missouri, were the highlights of the evening. The club presented a U.S. savings bond to Mrs. Ida White, Framingham, Massachusetts.

The Saturday, July 12 events included the following:

Picnic at Lincoln Park,
    Mrs. Mattye Foxx and Mr. Edward Gilmore in charge

Recreation:

1. *Bowling,* Mr. Lloyd Cole Beatty, chairman
2. *Golf,* Mr. Cecil W. Mitchell, chairman
   Mr. Byron Wilburn, Mr. Dee McGee, assistants
3. *Games,* S/Sgts. Alex and Reba Litman (Ret.)
4. *Dance by the Esquire Club*
   —Messrs. Charles Whitcomb and Phillip Berger
5. *Presentation of awards*
           a. Recreational events
           b. Person traveling greatest distance
           c. Oldest citizen
           d. Person with the largest family

The Sunday, July 13 events included:

Worship services at the Lincoln Center with Mr. Harold B. Wright, Kansas City, Missouri, introducing the Speaker: Reverend Elmer Newton. Mrs. Neva Cole Beatty and Miss Elvira Williams in charge.
Brunch, Mrs. Betty Scott and committee
Dinner, Mrs. Marie Toney and committee

The Officers:

President	Mrs. Catherine Berger
Vice-president	Mr. Lloyd Cole Beatty
Secretary	Mrs. Juanita Gilmore
Assistant secretary	Mrs. Marie Toney
Financial secretary	Mrs. Neva C. Beatty
Treasurer	Mrs. Marguerite Marshall
General program chairperson	Mrs. Glyncora Wilburn

Committees

Reception, Mrs. Darlene Mitchell, chairman;
    Mrs. Loyce Brown, Mrs. Carrie Jameison, Mr. Charles Dial, Sr., Mr. Miles Cole, Mrs. Francis McGraw, and Mrs. Barbara Williams

Queen-King Contest, Mrs. Mattye Foxx, chairman
    Mrs. Marguerite Marshall, assistant

Souvenir Program, Mrs. Claudine Caldwell, chairman
    Mrs. Dorice Beatty, Mr. Lloyd Beatty, Sr., Mr. Charles Dial, Jr., and Mr. Dee McGee

Golf Program, Mr. Cecil Mitchell, chairman
    Mr. Byron Wilburn and Mr. Dee McGee, assistants

Bowling, Mr. Lloyd Cole Beatty, chairman
    Mrs. Barbara Williams and Mrs. Dorice Beatty

Recreation, S/Sgts. Alex and Reba Litman (Ret.)

Picnic Lunch, Mrs. Mattye Foxx, chairman
    Messrs. Edward Gilmore, Andrew Foxx, Phillip Berger, Dee McGee, Mrs. Estella Kirk, Mrs. Darlene Mitchell, and Mrs. Marguerite Marshall

Dance, Esquire Club—Messrs. Charles Whitcomb and Phillip Berger

Brunch on Sunday, Mrs. Betty Scott, chairman
    Mr. Miles Cole, Mrs. Mattye Foxx, and Mrs. Darlene Mitchell

Worship Service, Mrs. Neva C. Beatty, chairman
    Miss Elvira Williams, Mrs. Mattye Foxx, Miss Johnnie Kaye Madison, Mrs. Betty Scott, Mr. Wesley Scott, Mr. C. B. Walker, Mr. Lloyd Beatty, Sr., and Mr. Charles Dial, Sr.

Dinner, Mrs. Marie Toney, chairman
    Assisting: Mrs. Hassie Mack, Mrs. Archieleen Greene, Mrs. Juanita Gilmore, Mr. Lloyd Beatty, Sr., and Mrs. Charles Dial, Jr.

Pianist, Mrs. Mattye Foxx
    Mr. Bobby Dismuke

News Reporter, Mrs. Glyncora Wilburn

Photographer, Mr. Cecil W. Mitchell

QUEEN   1975 KING

1st 1962
Judy Turner

2nd 1965
Mary Williams

3rd 1972
Marquerite Marshell

1st Runner Up
Juanita Gilmore

2nd Runner Up
Alice Marie Talbert

PITTSBURG HOMECOMING

Friday   July 11, 1975

LINCOLN CENTER

Registration   6:30 - 7:45 P.M.

PROGRAM - 8:00 P.M.

Negro National Anthem	Ms. Mattye Foxx, Pianist
Invocation	Elder Elzie Allmon
Welcome	Ms. Catherine Berger
Solo	Ms. Sandra Allmon
Introduction of Mayor	Ms. Darlene Mitchell
Welcome from the City of Pittsburg	Ms. Ruth Lemon, Mayor
Solo	Mr. Bobby D. Dismuke
Response	Mr. Delbert Jackson
Solo	Ms. Marri Margaret Woods
Introduction of Speaker	Mr. Thurston Graham
Speaker	Ms. Genevieve M. Shedrick
Solo	Ms. Marri Margaret Woods
Musical Interlude	Mr. Bobby J. Dismuke
King and Queen Coronation	Ms. Mattye Foxx
	Ms. Marguerite M. Marshall
Contestants	Chair Persons
	Sponsors
Skit	Mr. George R. Dismuke
Introduction of Officers	Ms. Loyce Brown
Remarks	Ms. Glyncora Wilburn
"THE BOND"	PRESENTATION
Benediction	Rev. Melvin Woods

RECEPTION

RECEPTION COMMITTEE

Ms. Darlene Mitchell, Chair Person	Ms. Carrie Jameison
Ms. Loyce Brown	Mr. Miles J. Cole
Ms. Barbara Williams	Mr. Charles Dial, Sr.
Ms. Frances McGraw	Mr. Lloyd Beatty

GREETERS

Mr. and Ms. Charles Greenlaw   Mr. and Mrs. James Giles

MORNING WORSHIP

Lincoln Center
July 13, 1975 - 10:45 A.M.

Devotionals - Mrs. Elzie Allmon, Mrs. Rosie Taylor, Mrs. Florence Martin and Mr. Charles Dial

Congregational Song ---------------------------- " Pass Me Not"

Scripture -------------------------------------- Rev. Henry . Pullum

Congregational Song ------------------------ "Guide My Oh Thy Great Jehovah"

Prayer --- Rev. L. W. Glenn

Music -- Community Choir

Offertory ----------- William Benefield, Benjamin White, Charles Whitcomb

Offertory Prayer ------------------------------ Elder Elzie Allmon

Soft Music ------------------------------------ Mrs. Mattye Fox, Pianist

Sweet In Memory

Karen Mack, Johnnie Kaye Madison, La Tawnya Gaines, Tracy Gaines, Lea Ann Scott, Deborah Pullman, Jeanny Blurton and Sharon Jackson.

Music -- Community Choir

Introduction of Speaker ----------------------- Mr. Harold Wright

Speaker -- Rev. Elmer Newton

Solo --- Mr. Andrew Foxx

Remarks -- Mrs. Catherine Berger, President

Chaoir and Congregation --------------------- "We'll Walk in the Light"

Benediction ----------------------------------- Rev. Elmer Newton

Chairman of Morning Service   Ushers - Chairman - Elvira Williams
   Neva Beatty   Melvin Foxx, Marvin Foxx
Chairman of Music   Darlene Blurton, Beatrice Blurton
   Mattye Foxx   Joyce Pullum and John Mack

SOUVENIR PROGRAM BOOKS DEDICATED
IN MEMORY OF OUR BELOVED FRIEND
CATHERINE BERGER

CATHERINE BERGER

YOUR MEMORY TO US IS A KEEPSAKE.
WITH WHICH WE WILL NEVER PART.
A PLACE IS VACANT THAT NEVER CAN BE FILLED.
A VOICE WE LOVED IS STILL.
THOUGH "GOD" HAS YOU IN HIS KEEPING,
WE WILL ALWAYS KEEP YOU IN OUR HEARTS.

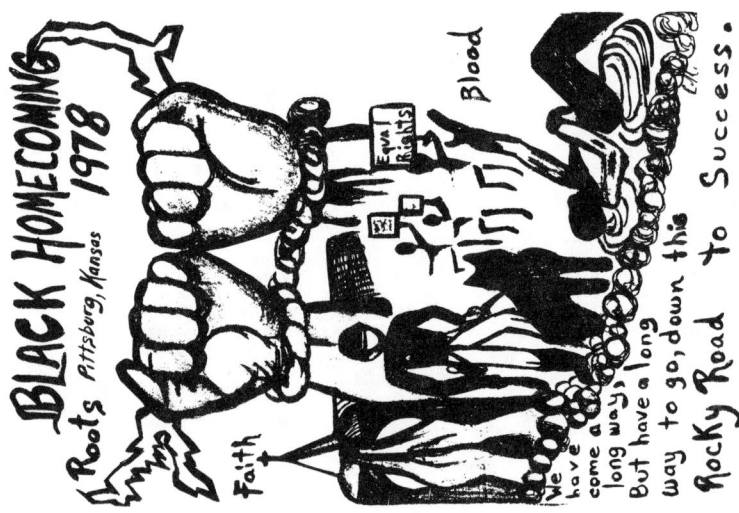

PROGRAM INFORMATION

King — M. Paul Summey
  Los Angeles, California
  Sponsor: Mrs. Florence Summey Nowling
  Los Angeles, California

Queen — Mrs. Rose Harris
  Pittsburg, Kansas
  Sponsor: Mrs. Juanita Gilmore
  Pittsburg, Kansas

First Runner-up Queen — Mrs. Maxine Boyd
  Humboldt, Kansas

Second Runner-up Queen — Mrs. Luberta Lenon
  Alexandria, West Virginia

  Sponsor: Sonja T. Lenon

Mrs. Betty Scott
Chairperson

Mrs. Marie Dorsey
C.-Chairperson

Pittsburg, Kansas
July 7, 1978

GREETINGS TO OUR FORMER PITTSBURG FRIENDS,

We, the members of the Homecoming Club, are delighted having you in Pittsburg.

Knowing that you were coming to help make this Homecoming another joyful occasion, has been exciting to us.

We hope all of you have a wonderful time.

THE PITTSBURG HOMECOMING CLUB AND MEMBERS

PITTSBURG HOMECOMING
THEME: "ROOTS, FAITH, BLOOD — SUCCESS"

Friday   LINCOLN CENTER   July 7, 1978

Registration .... Musical Interlude
7:40 - 8:00 p.m.

WELCOME PROGRAM — 8:00 p.m.

Negro National Anthem .. Ms. Secenia Scroggins - Pianist
Invocation .... Rev. LeRoy Nelson
Welcome .... Ms. Estella Kirk
Introduction of Mayor .... Ms. Darlene Mitchell
Welcome from the City
  of Pittsburg .... Ms. Sherry Strecker-Mayor
Solo .... Master Gregory Greene
Response .... Ms. Ida May Yolkum
King and Queen Coronation .... Ms. Beatty J. Scott
                                      Ms. Marie P. Dorsey
                                                        Chairperson
Ballet .... Miss Shelle Brown
Solo .... Master Gregory Greene
Introduction of speakers .... Ms. Evelyn Eagans
Speakers .... Roots - Mr. John Eason
                      Faith - Rev. Elmer Newton
                      Blood - Ms. Reba Litman
Musical Interlude .... Ms. Secenia Scroggins
Tribute to former teachers of Douglas School .. Ms. Elvira Williams
Recognition .... Ms. Neva Beatty
Introduction of Offiers .... Ms. Barbara Williams
Remarks by General Chrmn. .... Mattye Foxx
Dedication .... Youth Group
                DRAWING OF PRIZES
Benediction .... Rev. Henry M. Pullum
                   RECEPTION

GREETERS
Mr. and Mrs. Raymond Green
Mr. and Mrs. LeRoy Nowling
Mr. and Mrs. Raymond Martin

Queen   **King**

Rose Harris   Paul Summey

1st Runner Up   **2nd Runner Up**

Maxine Boyd   Luberta Lenon

NEGRO NATIONAL ANTHEM

Verses
1. LIFT EVERY VOICE AND SING,
   TILL EARTH AND HEAVEN RING,
   RING WITH THE HARMONY OF LIBERTY.

2. LET OUR REJOICING RISE,
   HIGH AS THE LIST'N'ING SKIES,
   LET IT RESOUND LOUD AS THE ROLLING SEA.

Chorus
SING A SONG, FULL OF THE FAITH THAT THE DARK PAST HAS TAUGHT US,
SING A SONG, FULL OF THE HOPE THAT THE PRESENT HAS BROUGHT US.
FACING THE RISING SUN, OF OUR NEW DAY BEGUN,
LET US MARCH ON, TILL VICTORY IS WON.

WELCOME PROGRAM, RECEPTION and DECORATING COMMITTEE

Ms. Darlene Mitchell, chairperson

Ms. Carrie Jameison	Ms. Barbara Williams
Ms. Mary Jane Clark	Ms. Loyce Poncil
Ms. Betty J. Scott	Ms. Marie P. Dorsey
Ms. Meridith Harris	Ms. Faye Smith
Ms. Carol Giles	Ms. Carol Kimbrough
Ms. Mary Ovesta Harris	Mr. Miles J. Cole
Mr. Lester Kirk	Mr. Charles Holley
Ms. Juanita Gilmore	Mr. Edward Gilmore

"PASS ME NOT"

1. Pass me not, O gentle Savior, Hear my humble cry while on others thou are calling, do not pass me by.
   Chorus: Savior, Savior, hear my humble cry while on others thou are calling, do not pass me by.

2. Thou, the Spring of all my comfort
   More than life to me
   Whom have I on earth beside thee?

"GUIDE ME O THOU GREAT JEHOVAH"

1. Guide me O thou Great Jehovah, Pilgrim thro' this barren land, I am weak, but Thou are mighty, Hold me with Thy powerful hand.
   Bread of heaven, Feed me till I want no more.
   Bread of heaven, Feed me till I want no more.

2. Open now the crystal fountain whence the healing waters flow, Let the fiery cloudy pillar lead me all my journey thro'; Strong Deliverer, be Thou still my strength and shield; Strong Deliverer, be Thou still my strength and shield.

On the Fifth Anniversary of the Pittsburg Homecoming Club
July 7–9, 1978

Theme: "Roots, Faith, Blood—Success"

On Friday, July 7, 1978, the president, Mrs. Estella Kirk, gave the welcome to those assembled, followed by the introduction of the mayor by Mrs. Darlene Mitchell. The mayor, Mrs. Sherry Strecker, of the city of Pittsburg. Mrs. Betty Scott and Mrs. Marie Dorsey held the audience spellbound with the king and queen coronation. The king, Mr. Paul Summey, Los Angeles, California; the queens, Mrs. Rose Harris, Pittsburg; Mrs. Luberta Lenon, Alexandria, Virginia; and Mrs. Maxine Boyd, Humboldt, Kansas. A response was given by Mrs. Ida Mae Yolkum, Washington, D.C. The speakers and their topics (introduced by Mrs. Evelyn Eagans):

Mr. John Eason, Kansas City, Missouri—	"Roots"
Reverend Elmer Newton, Kansas City, Missouri—	"Faith"
Mrs. Reba Litman, Lansing, Kansas—	"Blood"

Welcoming Committee:

Mr. and Mrs. Raymond Green, Los Angeles
Mr. and Mrs. LeRoy Nowling, Los Angeles
Mr. and Mrs. Raymond Martin, Oakland, Calif.

A tribute to the former teachers of the Frederick Douglass School was given by Miss Elvira Williams: Miss Irene Clem, Mrs. Neva Cole Beatty, and Mr. C. B. Walker.

Special Honor to Mr. Leroy Green, assistant professor of Computer Science, Temple University, Philadelphia, Pa.

The sports events and picnic highlighted the activities on Saturday, July 8, 1978.

Mrs. Audrey Scroggins, chairman of the Sunday morning worship services, had a beautiful program. Mr. Leroy Green had a "Time of Reminiscing," and Reverend Delphine Flowers was the speaker. Remarks and closing by the president, Mrs. Estella Kirk, after which dinner was served to approximately 400 people who were in attendance. The entire program was dedicated to the memory of our late president, Mrs. Catherine T. Berger.

Officers:

President	Mrs. Estella Kirk
Vice-President	Miss Elvira Williams
Secretary	Mrs. Juanita Gilmore
Assistant secretary	Mrs. Loyce Poncil
Financial secretary	Mrs. Neva C. Beatty
Assistant financial secretary	Mrs. Claudine Caldwell
Treasurer	Mrs. Marguerite Marshall
General program chairperson	Mrs. Mattye Foxx
Reception chairperson	Mrs. Darlene A. Mitchell
Picnic lunch	Mr. Andrew Foxx
Golf chairman	Mr. Cecil Mitchell
Youth sports	Mr. and Mrs. Alex Litman
Bowling	Mrs. Claudine Caldwell
Youth activities	Mrs. Barbara Williams
Dance Chairman	Mr. Edward Gilmore
Continental Breakfast	Mrs. Betty Scott
Sunday Worship Hour	Mrs. Audrey Scroggins
Sunday Dinner Chairman	Mrs. Marie Toney
Park Administrators	Mr. Edward Gilmore
	Mr. Ronnie Williams
Pianist	Miss Secenia Scroggins
	Mrs. Mattye Foxx
Cover of the Souvenir Program and Posters	Mrs. Rosaland Marshall

MORNING WORSHIP
Lincoln Center
July 9, 1978 - 10:45

Devotionals – Sis. Rose Taylor, Sis. Myrtle Wilson, Bro. Earnest Flowers
Time of Reminiscencing .... Prof. Leroy (Pap) Green
  (Author of Computer book "Introduction to BASIC and FORTRAN")
Processional .... Choir
Selection .... Choir
Greetings .... Sis. Kathryn Nelson
Scripture .... Rev. Louis Glenn
Prayer .... Eld. Virgil Watson
  (Mayor of Arkansas City, Kans.)
Selection .... Choir
Offertory Prayer .... Eld. Walter Dorsey
  (Soft music-Sis. Mattye Foxx)
Offering .. Bro. Nathan Benefield, Bro. Hugh Wilson, Bro.
  Jermiah Davis, and Bro. Ron Marshall
Solo .... Sis. Celestine Witcomb
  (In memory of her husband, Charles)

IN MEMORIAM

Chairperson .... Co-Chairperson
Sis. Florence Martin   Mother Ruth Allmon
Solo .... Sis. Juanita Gilmore
Introduction of speaker .... Sis. Celestine Witcomb
Solo .... Bro. Andrew Foxx
Speaker .... Minister Delphine Flowers
Invitation to discipleship .... Rev. Robert Docherty
Remarks .... Sis. Estella Kirk
                                           (President)
Choir and Congergation .... Walk In The Light
Benediction .... Rev. Henery Pullum
Chairperson .... Sis. Audrey Scroggins
Usher Chairman - Bro. Lester Kirk   Ushers: Sis. Marie Dorsey
Co-Chairman - Bro. Cecil Mitchell   Arlecia Scroggins
                                              Marvin Foxx

PRESIDENTS OF PITTSBURG HOMECOMING
GENERAL PROGRAM CHAIRPERSON

MILES J. COLE
1st Pres. 1962-1965

CATHERINE BERGER
2nd Pres. 1972-1975

ESTELLA KIRK
3rd Pres. 1978

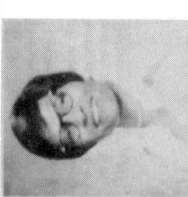

GLYNCORA WILBURN
1st General Program Chairperson
1962-1965   1972-1975

MATTYE FOXX
2nd General Program Chairperson
1978

The First Kansans: Bicentennial Celebration
1776-1976

We know that in 1541, the Kansas, Wichita, Pawnee and Comanche Indians lived here. They retained possession of the land when Vasquez de Coronado came seeking gold and, again, when La Salle came in 1682 on behalf of France. This West Louisiana territory was yielded by France to Spain in 1763. Spain retroceded to France in 1800 and in 1803, sold the Louisiana Purchase to the United States.

First Permanent Settlements were called "outposts" to protect travelers from Indian raids:

1. Fort Leavenworth, 1827
2. Fort Scott, 1842
3. Fort Riley, 1853

The passage of the Kansas-Nebraska Act, 1854, thrust Kansas into war—proslavery and antislavery forces—known at that time as "bleeding Kansas." The Jayhawkers won and, on January 29, 1861, entered the Union as a free state.

Thus, Kansas made the first step on life's highway to advance this new independence. Through hard work, hope, and perseverance, in keeping with the official motto: "Ad Astra per Aspera"—"To the stars through difficulty," these

Frontiersmen established towns, built
   homes, schools, businesses, and churches
   to enrich their new way of living;

                    and the
Farmers produced the food needed
   to help the early settlers survive;

later the
Factories and industries manufactured
goods and products that provided
Kansas economic security.

Today, Kansas is known as the "Nation's Breadbasket." The capital in Topeka was completed in 1903. There are 105 counties with a total population of 2,249,248 and ten cities whose population ranges from 263,297 to 25,927.

With this heritage, we may celebrate the Bicentennial by proudly singing our Official State Song: "HOME ON THE RANGE."

The Struggle for Existence in Kansas: How the Afro-American Family Mastered It

From our ancestors we inherited the stamina to sustain obstacles. You may ask how do we know these things? The answer is native instinct and understanding. Some of the outstanding obstacles we encountered for survival included:

  WEATHER   WORK   WISDOM

The first difficulty to overcome was the change of seasons. The *winters* brought severe snowstorms, ice, and freezing temperatures. This was hard on individuals, as it brought about many illnesses, and doctors were few and transportation almost lacking. The *springs* pelted rain, sometimes floods and frequent tornadoes in the area. This was a setback to the farmers, carpenters, corn and flour mills, and other occupations. The *summers* were sweltering with high temperatures. However, people managed to time their working hours for field chores; and, on weekends, have picnics, baseball games, and dancing. Sundays were spent with church services and with the family. The *fall* season was a happy time for everyone—harvest of crops, canning fruits and vegetables for family use during the winter, and best of all, the returning to school.

The second difficulty to overcome was locating employment after completing school that would offer economic security. The professional field had few vacancies, as those who were in it remained until age seventy or upward. Farming required acres and acres of land to be productive and an excess of money for equipment. Only a few industries in the area, and they were reducing their work force as time went by, such as—brickyards, coal mining, railroads, etc. Therefore, our only recourse was to seek employment elsewhere.

And this we did in order to fulfill our obligations to our families.

The third difficulty to deal with was how to pursue a course of life that would help us to assist our parents financially and to rear our immediate family. We had to make the choice, each individual in his own way, in order to become self-sufficient; and, most importantly, self-sustaining as we matured.

Today, the third and fourth generations consider this inheritance and wonder in amazement how our foreparents had the foresight to manage as they did. Our mother used to say, "We have to make both ends meet," in order to gain material wealth. That is to say, use what you have and stretch it to its capacity. For *both ends to meet,* the intention was threefold:

1. husband, wife, and children working and undertaking to pool their resources.
2. maintaining a savings account in a bank even though it was small.
3. purchase for the least amount of money only the necessities.

We accepted the teachings, guidance, and philosophy for living that they left us. And, with this background, we were able to subsist wherever we resided—in the city, suburb, or abroad—wherever our jobs were located.

We enriched our lives through these means:

1. love of home and family—by communicating with our parents through letters or telephone calls on a weekly basis.
2. love of church—contributing financially as well as physically.
3. sharing with others.
4. living a clean life in any community.
5. independence and self-confidence.
6. sacrificing to maintain our standards.

The above-mentioned means of survival for the Afro-American in Kansas is an attempt to bring forth the importance of families living together, sharing and receiving good moral habits.

The Afro-American Woman of Yesteryear in Kansas

Kansas became a state on January 29, 1861. This was four years prior to the adoption of the Thirteenth Amendment to the Constitution (December 18, 1865), ending slavery throughout the United States. Therefore, for years, the runaway slaves and the underground railroad were two ways of moving westward to seek freedom and the "Glory Road."

Dr. Earl Spangler states that "in 1879, Negroes from some of the deep Southern states started a mass exodus to Kansas and the West. Not all Negro leaders thought it wise to move.... They felt that the Negro would not be received with open arms in Kansas or other places."*

"Nicodemus Colony, U.S. 24, two miles west of Rooks-Graham County Line was founded by the Exodusters, groups of Negroes who homesteaded in Kansas in the 1870s. The first settlers arrived in 1877 and spent their first winter in dugouts and burrows. Never more than 500 strong, the community managed to produce a number of teachers, ministers, politicians and civil servants."†

"April, 1879, a Missouri River steamboat arrived at Wyandotte, Kansas, and discharged a load of colored men, women and children, with divers (sundry), barrels, boxes and bundles of household effects.... Not from any one State or section in particular, but from nearly all parts of the South."**

*Dr. Earl Spangler, *The Negro in America*. (Minneapolis, Minn.: Lerner Publications Company, 1969), pp. 33–34.

†American Oil Company (Now Amoco Oil Company), "American Traveler's Guide to Negro History," p. 15.

***Kansas Collection*—Rare Book. "A Year of the Exodus in Kansas," pp. 211–212."

Life was not easy for the Negro woman in Southeast Kansas from 1867 to 1967. Her destiny was threefold:

1. To perpetuate the family, and to maintain the ties
2. To help her children secure an education
3. To be gainfully employed in order to supplement the family budget.

In order to fulfill these duties, our mothers and our grandmothers had to be strong-willed, vigorous, and independent. Each was an indispensable person in the household, and through her efforts some economic security was attained.

Although our fathers worked—in the coal mines, the tile yards, brickyards, railroads, and as custodians for twelve to fourteen hours a day—they did not earn enough to support the family. Therefore, it was the mother who filled this gap in income by washing and ironing in her home. Other women served as maids in the white homes; some did cooking and sewing for white families. The early settlers in Kansas had little formal education and training. A few of the men were skilled artisans—blacksmiths, bricklayers, carpenters, cement finishers, horticulturists, and tailors—but found employment hard to secure; and apprenticeship and trade organizations would not accept them. Therefore, those who lacked the skills necessary to be selective worked with what they knew best.

In a taped interview in 1967, with one of our early settlers, she states:

> While the men worked in the mines the ladies would have a Church Circle that would meet in our homes. We would quilt, make doilies, tea towels, and other articles of clothing. We would sell them. Sometimes we cooked dinners and sold them for 25 cents a plate. This money was turned into the Circle, and when we had accumulated enough in the treasury we would divide it among the older people and widows to use as they saw fit.*

---

*The Crawford County Centennial, 1867–1967, pp. 31–32. An interview with Mrs. Flossie Slaughter, Croweburg, Kansas, July 24, 1967.

From another settler, we learn:

> The ladies prepared suppers and sold them. Chicken and ham sandwiches sold for 5 cents; dinners for 15 cents, and a quart of pop for 5 cents. The money was used for the upkeep of the church, that is, supplying coal oil lamps, tuning the organ, and the annual church picnic. For the picnic, the church would furnish pop and homemade ice cream. Each family brought baskets and would spread the food out on tables to share with others. The people came by hayrack. The games—baseball for the men, sewing and crocheting and visiting for the ladies, and the children played on swings or long-hanging wild grapevines. The socials were similar to the suppers.*

From 1880 to 1912, the public schools in Pittsburg were integrated, and the majority of the teachers were high school graduates or had received training in church schools. Some county schools were separate in Kansas at this time.

In 1912, we attended our first segregated school—The Frederick Douglass School. Here, an all-Negro faculty taught. The teachers were dedicated, and it was their philosophy to impart to each student a desire for learning. Therefore, our training was one that prepared for continued education or employment in the world of work. When we entered the senior high school, the situation was reverse—an all-White faculty. We were grouped in classes together—sewing, home economics, physical education, etc. Our table in the library (at study period time) was assigned, and it was the last one on the north side of the building. We were not members of extracurricular activities, nor did we participate in school assembly programs.

Upon entering college, the same situation applied. Negro students could not live in the dormitories; they were not permitted to practice teaching at Horace Mann School. To receive credit for the course, we had to walk to the Douglass School to do our practice teaching. Our swimming class was held at three P.M., on Friday, after the white students had

---

*An interview with Mrs. Rose Harris, April 26, 1973, Pittsburg, Kansas.

finished for the week. Again, the women had no extracurricular activities to perform, but the men did participate in athletics.

After completing college, job opportunities in Pittsburg were nil. Therefore, we left the city to find employment elsewhere.

From 1889 to 1939, the Negro woman held responsible positions in Pittsburg as:

Owners and managers of cafes and boarding homes
Dressmakers and designers
Home bakery and fancy candy shop
Fancy linen laundress
Farm managers
Music teachers in private homes

From 1940 to the present in Pittsburg, we find:

Nurses
Medical secretary
High school teachers
Social worker
Nursery school teachers
Public school teachers
Private industrial workers
Assistant children's librarian
Federal government employees
Caterer and assistant to the home economist,
    gas service company
Private home workers

From 1940 to the present, the women who left Pittsburg are in many diversified positions, which follow:

Director of Allied Health Division
Nurses
Hospital assistants and technicians
Musicians
Teachers
Owners of catering service
Restaurant owners
Rest and nursing home owner

Child care service
Government employees
Probation officer
School safety director
School counselors
Social workers
Beauticians
Dean of Women Students
Model and fashion designer
Tour guide
Saleswomen
Nursery school owner
Newspaper writer
Housewives and community workers

Summary

Prior to 1954, the status of the Negro woman in Kansas had been relegated to second-class citizenship. She was excluded from participating in community affairs and restricted in her personal contact with the whites. Because of this biased attitude, we encountered many obstacles on the road to progress.

Segregation caused the links of the chain to become weak by preventing interchange of cultures. However, as noted in the variety of categories of employment, one must admit that the capabilities of the Afro-American woman are no less than those of any other race.

As J. Saunders Redding, writer, critic, and teacher, said in an interview with Hollie I. West:

> Let me keep my identity, but don't restrict me. Don't make my blackness a penalty. I don't see how we can survive as a people unless we integrate.*

Edwin R. Embree speaks of the plight of the Negro thusly:

---

*Hollie I. West, The *Washington Post*, 10 January 1971, K Section, 1–5.

So with our right hand, we raise to high places the great who have dark skins. And, with our left, we slap them down to "keep them in their place."*

The early settlers came to Kansas with good minds, strong bodies, and a will to work. We are the heirs to these qualities. And it is our desire to encourage future generations to preserve this heritage since these are the attributes that develop good citizens, happy homes, and strong leadership.

---

*Edwin R. Embree, *American Negroes: A Handbook.* (New York: John Day Company, now Thomas Y. Crowell Company, 1948), p. 50.

A Most Remarkable Person

It was Sunday, July 9, 1967, and the family had assembled at home for a quiet celebration with our parents on the occasion of their fifty-eighth wedding anniversary. On July 12, 1959, we had a formal affair for their fiftieth anniversary, and they enjoyed it.

After dinner, mother and father opened the gifts with such exclamations as "Why did you do it?" "It is just what I need," and "Thanks to all." The highlight of the day for mother was the presenting of a cake, decorated with the words, "Happy 58th Anniversary to Emily and Levi," by their fishing friends, Mr. and Mrs. Ray Lowe.

Mother's eyes simply danced as she accepted the box and said: "I don't know why you are always giving us presents."

Mrs. Lowe replied: "We count you two as our very dear friends. Such a special occasion as this—fifty-eight years of peace and harmony with a family—merit friends showing their respect by thinking about you and giving gifts."

Upon opening the box, mother excitedly said; "Oh, Levi just look! Isn't it beautiful? It is too pretty to cut. One would just love to keep it forever to remember this day. However, since the children are here, I guess we will have to share it with them."

Mr. Lowe proclaimed: "Now, Emily, be sure you get the largest piece because Levi's 'sweet tooth' is acting up again."

Emily replied: "Don't you worry about that, Mr. Lowe; only upon written permission to me will this cake be cut."

Levi responded by saying, "I guess I had better start writing a 'permission' note now because I usually have a midnight snack and will be counting on a slice of cake at that time."

With this remark, everyone laughed, and the Lowes left. The family returned to the dinner and gifts.

The Family:

Mother: Mrs. Emily Fonchoser Mitchell
Father: Mr. Henry Levi Mitchell
Brother and Wife: Cecil and Darlene A. Mitchell
Sister and husband: Genevieve and Wilbur Shedrick
Sister and husband: Ida Mae and William Yolkum and Daughter, Antoinette
Sister and husband: Marguerite M. and Ulysses Marshall

50th wedding anniversary of Henry Levi and Emily Mitchell, July 12, 1959. *Left to right:* Ulysses, Marguerite, William, little Antoinette, Ida, Emily, Henry Levi, Genevieve, Wilbur, Darlene, and Cecil.

A Most Remarkable Man

You ask, "What makes your family feel that your father was a remarkable man?"

Our reply—"He was honest; he was a firm believer in hard work; and, he had respect for all human beings."

His honesty was revealed in his ability to work on one job for thirty years without being late, absent, or negligent. Also, in the ability to serve the store in several capacities—warehouse clerk, distributor of merchandise to each department, a window decorator, and each year acting as Santa Claus for the store. The Pittsburg *Headlight* carried an article on March 1, 1938, stating that "Levi Mitchell is at home with an attack of influenza. Mr. Mitchell has been absent from work three times in 28 years."

The hard work included twelve to fourteen hours on the job for six days a week to support the family. Upon coming home, he did repairs around the home, helped the children with homework assignments, planted a garden of fruits and vegetables, and on Sundays attended church, where he served as a Deacon. No job was ever too difficult for him; if he once tackled it, he continued until it was completed. In his spare time, he pursued home-study courses in electricity and was able to assist the electrician with new fixtures and plugs in our home when we moved in 1923 to the West Forest area. We never heard our father say he was too tired to do a task.

After retiring from Ramsay's, he continued to work at Hull & Dillon Packing House until 1965. Other activities included serving as secretary for Golden Gate Lodge, No. 66; as a deacon in the church, and maintaining the rental property that he owned.

In his respect for human beings, we find it in the love that he generated to his family and the capacity to venerate a portion of this love to all mankind. I would say that he was a Christian because he always found good points in the lives of the people with whom he worked, served, or came in contact. Anyone with a problem could rely on him to give them a positive and truthful answer. As children, we were taught by him that "every tub must stand on its own bottom." This meant self-reliance, independence, and persistence. Towards this end, the four children have worked to uphold the standards that he set.

The Gift of Growing a Garden
by Cecil W. Mitchell and Ulysses Marshall

A farmer's work is compared to that of an artist in that he must apply himself to accomplish an end result. The steps a farmer takes form a seasonal pattern. The steps an artist takes form a refined pattern. Both have inherent tendencies that nature supplied.

A FARMER	AN ARTIST
in the winter, makes a compost bed, checks his seeds, and *outlines* planting	prepares his *easel*; selects paints to be used, and makes a *sketch*
in the spring, must plow, harrow, and cultivate the *land*; sows seeds, waters the plants, and *controls* the weeds	begins painting the *outline* will *remove* unnecessary designs
in the summer, *harvests*, markets, and shares produce	*finishes* the *picture*
in the fall, portrays his naturalist tendencies by *canning*, *storing*, *drying*, and *preserving* the crops.	*frames* his completed work

Joy, satisfaction, and a gleam of light will fill the eyes of the artist and the farmer when each beholds the beauty of the scene. What is this gift of growing a garden? you ask. Our answer—"It is patience, understanding, and a love of seeing plants grow and thrive."

Garden vegetables grown by Ulysses Marshall

People Whom I Admire for the Contribution They Made to Our Society

First and foremost on my list would be my family. Our father, Henry Levi Mitchell (1887–1971), set a goal for his life—to work to support the family and to educate his children—which he did fulfill. For thirty-two years, he was employed at Ramsay's and for twenty years at the Hull and Dillon Packing Company. He was satisfied when the children were grown and all employed.

Our mother, Emily J. Fonchoser Mitchell (1890–1973), was a genius in her ability to cook the humblest of foods and make them palatable. We always looked forward to our Sunday dinners when we were growing up at home, and she always prepared everything before going to church. To recall her specialty would be hard to do, but the doctors, lawyers, etc., who went hunting, brought their quail, ducks, pheasants, and geese for her to cook. While employed at the Gas Service Company as assistant home economist with Mrs. Ellen Bridges, home economist, mother prepared the meats, fish, fowl, salads, and desserts, that everyone enjoyed immensely. The four children—a brother, Cecil, worked for twenty years at the Spencer's Chemical Plant, and is currently assistant supervisor of the maintenance department at Kansas State University, Pittsburg. His wife, Darlene Adkins Mitchell, is a medical assistant secretary for a heart specialist-doctor. A sister, Genevieve, is a retired teacher from the Dawson, Georgia, public school system. Her husband, Wilbur Shedrick, is an aide at the nursing home in Dawson, Georgia. Another sister, Ida Mae, is a nurse at the Department of Human Resources, Aid to Dependent Children

Division, Washington, D.C. Her husband, William Yolkum, is a retired army serviceman. They have one daughter, Antoinette, who is married to Benjamin Brown; and they have two daughters, Knachia and Emileta Brown. The oldest sister, and writer of this article, is a retired counselor from the Washington, D.C. public school system. Her husband, Ulysses Marshall, is a retired U.S. Atomic Energy Commission top secret control officer.

Dr. Lewis Napier Bass, Sr.

He and his wife, Mrs. Mary F. Bass, came to Pittsburg, Kansas, from Iola, Kansas, in 1920. Dr. Bass applied at the county seat in Girard, Kansas, for his license to practice medicine in Kansas and immediately opened his office at 120 East 11th Street.

At this time, the physician made house calls. If a family did not have a telephone, someone would walk to the office to inform the doctor. Many times, a neighbor or a person on his way to work assumed this responsibility since the family could not go to the office.

Dr. Bass, a very sympathetic and understanding individual, had a talent for making one feel well. This was accomplished by the soft tone of his voice, his encouraging words, and, last but not least, the medicine he prescribed. During the 1920s, there was an epidemic of influenza, and this kept him busy. Other medical assistance that he performed in the community included the usual outbreak of children's diseases, casualties of the men working in the coal mines, brick, and tile yards, and taking care of the infirmities of the elderly. He served the community for forty-five years, retiring in 1965.

In 1967, he and Mrs. Bass moved to Seattle, Washington, to be with their children.

On October 27, 1978, Mrs. Mary F. Bass expired in Seattle and was interred at Highland Cemetery in Iola, Kansas.

Mr. Otto Alexander (son of Mrs. Mary Alexander of Pittsburg, Kansas) visiting with Dr. Lewis N. Bass, Sr., 1974

Dr. Lewis Napier Bass, Sr., and his wife, Mrs. Mary F. Bass. Seattle, Washington, 1974.

Dr. Bass still resides in Seattle along with three of his children and their families:

His daughter and son-in-law
    Mr. Perry and Mrs. Harriet Bass Thomas
Twin sons and daughters-in-law:
    Mr. Robert and Mrs. Nadean Bass
    Mr. Roscoe and Mrs. Zeola Bass
Another son and daughter-in-law:
    Dr. Lewis Napier Bass, Jr., and Mrs. Nadine Bass reside in Shawnee Mission, Kansas.
There are eleven grandchildren
    and two great grandchildren:
Grandchildren:
- Lewis Bass, III
- Andrea Bass
- Paula Bass
- Rosalyn Bass
- Roscoe Bass, Jr.
- Sheryl Bass
- Mary Bass
- Robert Bass, Jr.
- David Bass
- Michael Thomas
- Lynne Thomas

Great grandchildren
- Kim
- Tanisha

Mr. Neil Pierce, Sr.

He was born May 4, 1978, in Baxter Springs, Kansas, and came to Pittsburg, Kansas, in 1894. On June 22, 1905, he married Susie B. Weaver, and they resided at 312 West Forest. Their home was always open to the college students for meetings, social gatherings, and entertaining other campus friends or members of their families.

Mr. Pierce was active in local commerce, spending more than thirty-two years of his life with the Pittsburg Wholesale Grocery Company, first as a shipping clerk and later as their coffee roaster. When the wholesale grocery company became bankrupt during the Depression years of the "thirties," Neil Pierce started his own coffee business. Neil's Coffee Business attended to the roasting and blending of several kinds of coffee for his customers throughout Crawford County. He retired in 1948.

Neil Pierce, Sr., was best known for his work in the Masonic Lodge, having been a grand officer for over twenty-five years. He was a member of the Golden Gate Lodge #66 of Masons, Masonic chapter, Masonic commandery, and the Coran Temple of Kansas City; a member of the Elks, the 100F Lodge; the first all-black Payne's military band; and a member of Bethel A.M.E. Church. He died April 13, 1952.

Neil and Susie increased their family with two children: a daughter, Miss Marjorie Louise Pierce, served as Dean of Women at Langston University, Langston, Oklahoma, until her death October 2, 1959. Miss Pierce taught at the Fredrick Douglass School, Pittsburg, Kansas; at Fort Scott, Kansas, and Joplin, Missouri.

A son, Mr. Neil Pierce, Jr., and his wife, Delvet Haynes Pierce, reside in Oklahoma City, Oklahoma. Mr. Pierce retired in 1975 from the Oklahoma City public school system after serving as industrial arts teacher, principal, and, in 1963, as special assistant researcher for the Oklahoma City Board of Education.

Second Lieutenant William M. Benefield, Jr.

Second Lieutenant William M. Benefield, Jr., son of Mr. William M. Benefield, Sr., and Mrs. Samantha Benefield, was born June 23, 1926 in Pittsburg, Kansas. He completed his education here and was planning to become a doctor but decided on a military career instead.

Serving as a platoon leader, 77th Combat Engineer Company, 24th Infantry Regiment, 25th Infantry Division in the Republic of Korea, he was killed on July 29, 1950 while trying to remove an enemy mine field under fire. The Distinguished Service Cross, Silver Star, and Purple Heart were awarded (posthumously) in 1950. On November 16, 1975, the dedication ceremony of the William M. Benefield, Jr., United States Army Reserve Center was held in Pittsburg, Kansas. His wife, Mrs. Carrie Benefield, unveiled the plaque-portrait. Dr. Dudley T. Cornish was the dedication speaker.

Besides his parents, Mr. and Mrs. William M. Benefield, Sr., other members include:

A sister and brother-in-law:
    Mrs. Katye Benefield Johnson
    and Mr. Louvoid L. Johnson,
        teachers in the Tulsa, Oklahoma public school system

A brother:
    the late Mr. Adolph Benefield,
    Hollywood, California—January 18, 1978.

The family of Second Lieutenant Benefield include:

His wife,
    Mrs. Carrie Benefield,
    nurse, Washington, D.C.

A daughter,
    Miss Karen Benefield,
    probation officer, Washington, D.C., Public School System

Two sons and daughters-in-law:
    Mr. Michael and Mrs. Paulette Benefield and son.
    Mr. Michael Benefield is employed as state manager for Church's Chicken Restaurants for Ohio, Indiana, and Illinois.
    Mr. Steven and Mrs. Stephanie Benefield:
    Mr. Steven Benefield is employed by the Washington, D.C. Police Department, and also serves as a basketball coach for youngsters in the area.

Dedication

William M. Benefield Jr.

United States

Army Reserve Center

Nov. 16, 1975

2:00 P.M.

Lt. William M. Benefield, Jr., 1945

2LT William M. Benefield, Jr. was born 23 June 1926. Lieutenant Benefield distinguished himself with extraordinary heroism in action while serving as a Platoon Leader 77th Combat Engineer Company, 24th Infantry Regiment, 25th Infantry Division in the Republic of Korea. He was awarded the Distinguished Service Cross, Silver Star and Purple Heart (Posthumous). Before entering the Armed Forces, William attended Pittsburg High School and later Kansas State College of Pittsburg. He was planning on being a Doctor but decided on a military career. He was held in high esteem by all who knew him. We are indeed fortunate to have such a man from this community, honored by his country for which he gave his life, to be honored further by perpetuating his name with this memorial.

PROGRAM

Rendition of Honors .... 89th US Army Reserve Command
Bi-Centennial Color Guard

Invocation .... Rev. Louis Glenn, Pastor
New Hope Baptist Church
Pittsburg, Kansas

National Anthem .... Pittsburg High School Trumpeteers

Introduction of Military .... Master of Ceremonies
and Civilian Dignitaries   Maj. James M. AuBuchon
HQ, 243d S/S BN

Welcome and Introduction .... Mayor Ruth Lemon
of Guest Speaker   Pittsburg, Kansas

Dedication Speaker .... Dr. Dudley T. Cornish

Remarks .... Maj. Daniel R. Nance
CDR, 1010th S/S CO

Memorialization Ceremony

    Eulogy .... Charles T. Whitcomb
Girard, Kansas

    Reading of General Order ...... Master of Ceremonies

    Plaque-Portrait Unveiling .... Ms. Carrie Benefield

Remarks .... Master of Ceremonies

Benediction .... Mr. Lloyd Beatty, Chaplain
Post 158, American Legion

Robert C. Caldwell,
Kansas State representative,
District 68

Mr. Robert C. Caldwell

A native Pittsburger whom we all admire is Mr. Robert C. Caldwell. We hold him in esteem for the contributions that he made to his country. His accomplishments include:

Served as lieutenant in the European theater of operation during World War II;

Served as city commissioner, Salina, Kansas;

For thirty-nine years, he worked as a graphic arts teacher at the Salina, Kansas, high school;

Completed three terms as mayor of Salina (the first Afro-American to become mayor of that city);

In 1975, he was elected to the Kansas Legislature as state representative from the 68th District. He continues to perform his duties as scoutmaster of Troop 8. (This he has done for 38 years.)

Civic and professional interests occupy his time. Mr. Caldwell is currently working on legislation involving the improvement of the educational process.

Mr. Caldwell's family include:

His wife,
- Mrs. Bessie Ellis Caldwell, associate professor of physical education, Marymount College, Salina

Two daughters and a son-in-law:
- Dr. Aqualyn T. Caldwell Colbert, professor of psychology, Emporia State University, Emporia, Kansas; and her husband, Dr. Charles C. Colbert, assistant to the president of Emporia State University, Emporia, Kansas; Miss Teree Caldwell, pre-law senior at Spelman College, Atlanta, Georgia

Harold Wright

Mr. Harold B. Wright

We also admire another native Pittsburger, Mr. Harold B. Wright, for his understanding of and devotion to improving humanity.

Mr. Wright started his teaching career in 1940 in Weir, Kansas. This was interrupted because of his entrance into the armed forces. From 1942 to 1945, he served in military installations in Australia, New Guinea, and the Philippine Islands. After the war, he returned to his teaching post at Northeast Junior High School, Kansas City, Kansas. His assignments here included that of varsity basketball coach, athletic director, physical education department, varsity track coach, seventh grade basketball coach, director of intramural sports, instructor, health and physical education, and director of book rental. He retired June 30, 1975.

He and his wife, Mrs. Hazel Wright, enjoy traveling and caring for his mother, Mrs. Josephine Wright Strong. His sister, Mrs. Leah W. Boone, is a teacher in Kansas City; her husband, Mr. William W. Boone, is the principal of Northeast Junior High School, Kansas City, Kansas; Mrs. Eunice W. Ward and her husband, Dr. Arthur Ward, also teach in Baton Rouge, Louisiana. The father, Mr. Arthur N. Wright, was employed for many years at the Elks Club. He and a son, Mr. Marvin Wright, are deceased.

Dr. Hazle W. Blakeney

A native of Pittsburg, Dr. Blakeney received the B.S. degree from Kansas State University, Pittsburg, Kansas, and the masters and doctorate of education degrees in administration and teaching in schools of nursing from Teachers College, Columbia University, New York.

She is the daughter of the late Rev. John R. and Mrs. Vallie Love Walker. At the Good Samaritan Hospital School of Nursing, Charlotte, North Carolina, she served as staff nurse, supervisor, assistant director of nursing to director of nursing service and nursing education. After leaving North Carolina, Dr. Blakeney became director of the Allied Health Division of Essex County College in Newark, New Jersey.

Other activities that she engages in include: workshops relative to nursing; attendance at conferences; serving as speaker for many organizations and helping with community and civic projects that embrace health.

Dr. Blakeney is presently serving as professor of nursing education and administration at the University of Maryland, College Park, Maryland.

Mrs. Mattie E. Spottswood

Mrs. Mattie E. Spottswood, a native Washingtonian, selected teaching in the Washington, D.C., public school system as her career. Probationary teachers were assigned to her classroom for observation of methods and techniques at the Morgan Demonstration School. Mrs. Spottswood is efficient, thorough, and well organized for whatever task she must perform. Her understanding of the educational process and devotion to teaching enables her to help others to become proficient. She encourages each child to develop pride in worthwhile accomplishments, to acquire self-confidence, and to set and attain goals. She receives support from parents and community to help make the school setting a happy one for pupils.

After leaving the Morgan School, Mrs. Spottswood was appointed principal of the Charles Young Elementary School. Here, she works with an assistant principal, thirty-four classroom teachers, ten specialists, a librarian, two counselors, a school nurse, lunchroom clerks, the office staff, and the custodial staff. She operates an efficient school with the cooperation and teamwork afforded by the staff.

Dr. George Washington Carver

The next person on my list is Dr. George Washington Carver (1860–1943) because of his unique contribution to science and his highly trained scientific mind. His experimenting with the peanut plant gave us insight into the food value it contained and the hundreds of by-products that he developed from the peanut. The recipes below are the results of his work.

SPICY PEANUT BUTTER AND RAISIN BUNDT CAKE

½ cup peanut butter
2 cups sugar
4 eggs
4½ cups sifted flour
½ teaspoon salt
1 cup raisins
½ cups butter or margarine
1½ cups apple butter
2 cups buttermilk
2 teaspoons baking powder
2 teaspoons baking soda

In a bowl mix peanut butter and butter until fluffy. Stir in sugar. beat in eggs, one at a time, beating well after each addition. Stir in apple butter and buttermilk. Add remaining ingredients. Beat until well blended. Pour mixture into a greased and floured bundt cake pan or a 10 × 4-inch tube pan. Bake in a preheated 350-degree oven for one hour and fifteen minutes.

Cool in pan for 5 minutes, tap to loosen, and unmold on a cake rack. Dust with confectioners' sugar.

FRENCH TOASTED PEANUT BUTTER SANDWICH

1 Loaf of French or Italian bread, 14" long
1 cup peanut butter
2 cups well-drained sliced fruit—bananas, peaches, apricots (or use fresh canned or frozen)
2 eggs
1 cup milk
1 tablespoon sugar
1 teaspoon vanilla
¼ cup butter or margarine
¼ cup peanut oil

Cut bread with a serrated knife into ¾" thick diagonal slices. Spread half of the slices with peanut butter. Top peanut butter with fruit. Top with remaining bread slices. In a bowl, beat eggs with milk, sugar, and vanilla. Dip sandwiches into egg mixture, using slotted spoon or spatula. Heat butter and oil in a large skillet or griddle and fry sandwiches until golden brown on both sides. Serve warm. Makes six servings.

Sara Breedlove Walker

I admired Sara Breedlove (Madame C. J.) Walker (1867–1919) for her ingenuity in developing cosmetic products that enhanced the beauty of the Afro-American woman. She was the first Afro-American woman to become a millionaire. Her motto "The key to happiness and success is a good appearance," caused her to be the financial genius that she was.

Sara Breedlove Walker
(Madam C. J. Walker)
1867-1919

A financial genius who became one of America's first black woman millionaires.

Sarah Breedlove, who was later to become known as Madam C. J. Walker, was born in a shack in Delta, Louisiana in 1867. Orphaned early, she was raised by an older sister. When she was 14, she married C. J. Walker and by the age of 20, Sarah was a widow.

In 1887 Sarah took her little girl, A'Lelia, to St. Louis. For the next 18 years, Sarah worked as a washerwoman. Worried about what would happen when she could no longer bend over soapy tubs, Madam Walker had a dream in 1905 which told her to start the business which led her to fame and wealth.

The business was the sale of cosmetics. No one knows her original formula for a hair straightener, but traveling to Denver, she began selling her product door-to-door. At that time kinky African hair was considered a stigma, so Madam Walker's product was considered a miracle.

She soon expanded to a mail order operation. By 1913, her company was incorporated, had a foreign department operating in four languages, had franchised Madam C. J. Walker Beauty Shops across the country and was the largest business in the United States owned and operated by blacks.

In 1913, Madam Walker built a town house in New York City at Lenox Avenue and 136th Street. Her daughter, A'Lelia, became Harlem's first black debutante. Many prominent black and white guests were entertained there.

Black architect V. W. Tandy built her mansion at Irvington-on-Hudson. The estate which cost almost half a million dollars was christened "Villa Lewaro" by the great Italian tenor, Enrico Caruso. Madam Walker died in 1919 shortly after Villa Lewaro was completed.

However, her critics claim that Madam's success was possible because she kowtowed to the white man's image of beauty. They contend that her elaborately written *Madam C. J. Walker Beauty Manual* never mentioned the real aim of her product — which was hair straightening.

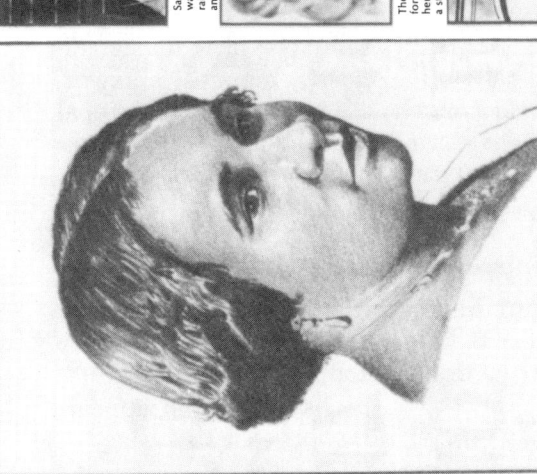

Personally humble, Madam Walker was a devout member of the African Methodist Church. Her last will stipulated that two-thirds of the net income from her estate would go to black charities. She provided recreational facilities for her employees and stressed strict courtesy in her shops.

Today her company is automated. The Madam C. J. Walker Colleges and Shops are independently owned and regardless of hair style or skin tone, her maxim is still used: "The key to happiness and success is a good appearance."

Some of her products are still being manufactured and sold. They are as follows:

HAIR CARE PRODUCTS
  Glossine
    Shampoo
    Scalp ointment
    Soap
    Pressing oil

SKIN AND FACIAL PRODUCTS
  Soap
    Cold cream
    Powder, various shades
    Rouge
    Lipstick

MISCELLANEOUS PRODUCTS
Combs, hair brushes, curlers, and other cosmetic articles.

Duke Ellington

Edward (Duke) Ellington (1899–1974) for his cultural offering to our society. He was a renowned composer, conductor, and pianist. Some of his outstanding musical compositions include the following numbers:

"Black, Brown and Beige"
"Satin Doll"
"Sophisticated Lady"
"In My Solitude"
"Mood Indigo"
"In a Sentimental Mood"
"I Let a Song Go Out of My Heart"
"Just Sitting and Rocking"

Besides composing jazz, blues, and classical music, Ellington also did several religious concerts, his most noteworthy being a sacred music concert, 1965, at Grace Episcopal Cathedral in San Francisco. "Nine hundred published pieces of his music range from classical, popular, sacred, symphonies and mood music."*

Representative Barbara Jordan

"Representative Barbara C. Jordan, born February 21, 1936 in Houston, Texas. B.A. degree from Texas Southern University (magna cum laude); Boston University School of

---

*Shaw-Barton, George Beach, Inc. "The American Negro Commemorative Society, Inc." Philadelphia, Pennsylvania, 1977.

Texas Congresswoman Barbara Jordan

Law, J.D., 1959. Practicing attorney, Texas Senate 1966–1972, president pro-tem, executive committee of National Democratic Committee."*

Representative Jordan, elected to the Congress of the United States from the 18th District in Texas, became service connected on January 3, 1973. She is an outstanding speaker, serving as the keynote speaker for the 1976 Democratic National Convention. With this speech, the nation became aware of Representative Jordan's integrity, profound knowledge of the political process, and her conscientiousness.

"Representative Barbara C. Jordan (D), 18th District in Texas, is the majority leader on the Committee on Govern-

*Charles B. Brownson, *1976 Congressional Staff Directory* (Congressional Staff Directory, Mount Vernon, Virginia, 1976), p. 106.

ment Operations; Sub-Committee on Intergovernmental Relations and Human Resources; Sub-Committee on Administrative Laws and Governmental Relations; and the Democratic Steering and Policy Committee."* Her major legislative achievements enacted into law have been:

Amendments to the Voting Rights Acts
Repeal of federal authorization for state "fair trade" laws
Mandatory civil rights enforcement
Procedures for the Law Enforcement Assistance Administration
    and the Office of Revenue Sharing.†

Dr. Mordecai Wyatt Johnson

On June 30, 1926, Dr. Mordecai Wyatt Johnson was selected as the 13th president of Howard University in Washington, D.C., the first Negro president of Howard.

Dr. Johnson was born January 12, 1890, in Paris, Tennessee. After completing high school at Howe Institute in Memphis, Tennessee, he enrolled in the Atlanta Baptist College and graduated in 1911 with honors. He received the bachelor of arts degree in 1913 from the University of Chicago; the bachelor of divinity degree in 1920 from Rochester, New York Theological Seminary; and the master of sacred theology degree in 1922 from Harvard University. His father, Wyatt Johnson, was the founder and pastor of the Mt. Zion Baptist Church in Paris, Tennessee.

In his inaugural address on June 10, 1927, he stated:

> Howard University is one among many agencies working for the development of the Negro people and for that enlargement of the life of our country which must *inevitably* follow every step of

Ebony Magazine, Johnson Publishing Company, Chicago, Illinois, August 1977, p. 91.

†*Ebony Magazine*, August 1977, p. 91. Johnson Publishing Company, Chicago, Illinois 60605.

this development.... I hope that during my administration Howard University may prove an increasingly worthy cooperator in our great common undertaking.*

He retired from Howard University in 1960, and his Howard years ended with rites in the Andrew Rankin Chapel on September 14, 1976.

Marian Anderson
(Contralto)

Marian Anderson was born on February 27, 1902 in Philadelphia, Pennsylvania. At the age of nineteen, she appeared as soloist with the New York Philharmonic. She is admired for the beautiful contralto voice that gives meaning to the songs and music that she renders. The spirituals—our Afro-American heritage—always bring tears to your eyes when she sings them. It was in 1939 that Miss Anderson gave her most memorable concert from the steps of the Lincoln Memorial in Washington, D.C., after being denied the privilege of singing at Constitution Hall by the DAR.

In 1955, she made her Metropolitan debut in Verdi's *The Masked Ball*. In September 1958, Miss Anderson was named to the U.S. delegation to the United Nations.

On August 28, 1963, Miss Anderson was a participant in the program "March On Washington." She lives with her husband, Orpheus Fisher, in Danbury, Connecticut.

Dr. Sterling A. Brown

Born in Washington, D.C., in 1901, Professor Brown was educated at Williams College and at Harvard, graduating with Phi Beta Kappa honors. As a writer, lecturer, drama critic, and professor of American literature at Fisk, Howard, and

*Michael R. Winston, Comp. Moorland-Springarn Research Center, Howard University, 1976, p. 20.

Lincoln (Missouri University), he is unsurpassed.

His lectures embrace the key to "mind building": 1) to read, 2) listen to stories told by others, and 3) write these ideas down for their historical importance. His poem entitled "Strong Men" is very significant in that it is the history of the Afro-American people.

HONORARY DOCTORATE DEGREES AWARDED:

In 1971, Howard University
University of Massachusetts
In 1973, Northwestern University
In 1974, Boston University
Williams (his *alma mater*)
Brown University
In 1975, Lewis and Clark.

His wife, Mrs. Daisy Turnbull Brown, is a literary person in her own right. They reside in Washington, D.C.

Dr. Eva Jessye

Standing tall on the stage of the Carney Hall Auditorium, attired in a long, black evening dress, is a native Kansan, Dr. Eva Jessye. On this occasion, the performance of her folk oratorio of "Paradise Lost and Regained," she became the recipient of the recognition that she so rightly deserved. The recognition received from the governor of the state of Kansas, Mr. Robert Bennett, was the declaration of October 1 as Eva Jessye Day throughout the state.

Many other expressions of appreciation were also presented to Dr. Jessye by friends, the cast, James Appleberry, president of Pittsburg State University, and the Pittsburg Arts Council.

At the end of the performance, which Dr. Jessye had written, directed, and conducted, the audience gave a stand-

'Paradise' premieres Sunday

The midwest premiere of Dr. Eva Jessye's "Paradise Lost and Regained" will be the most complete production ever performed of the folk oratorio.

Dr. Jessye, 83, will direct and conduct the program at 3 p.m. Sunday in Carney Auditorium. The event will be one of the highlights of the PSU 75th Anniversary Diamond Jubilee observance.

Kansas Gov. and Mrs. Robert Bennett will fly to Pittsburg for the performance. He will declare Oct. 1 as Eva Jessye Day throughout the state.

President Jimmy Carter will be represented at the performance by Dr. Walter Anderson, director of the music program at the National Endowment for the Arts. Also coming will be William Warfield and others who worked with Dr. Jessye when she was choral director for such shows as "Porgy and Bess," "Four Saints in Three Acts" and "Hallelujah."

"Paradise Lost and Regained" is known as a folk oratorio because traditional spirituals are used to highlight and illustrate the poetic narration of John Milton's 24-volume work.

The 1972 premiere at Washington Cathedral utilized only choirs, organ and dancers. Dr. Jessye says that the fully instrumented and technically produced PSU show "is the culmination of a dream."

Dr. Jessye was born in 1895 at Coffeyville. Her father was an outlaw, but she created a much different reputation for herself, becoming known as a poet, journalist, musician and humanist. She directed the official choir for the 1963 Martin Luther King Civil Rights March on Washington, and at memorial services held each year since that time.

Marshall Turley is coordinator of choirs for the PSU production. Carolann Martin is conductor of the string orchestra, with Gary Corcoran as brass choirs director and M. Evelyn Triplett as dance director.

Barry Bengtsen is set design and technical director, and Linda Vollen did the costumes for the production. Paul R. Lawrence has been in charge of sound and recording. The stage crew is composed of persons from the PSU music and speech and theatre departments.

Soloists for the program will be Carol Cook, Mel Bowie, Bonnie Poulos, Robert Docherty, Irelene Swain, Robert Smith, Ruby Stewart, Robert Moore, James Kindall, Lemuel Sheppard, William Vance, Robert Diskin, Myron Higerd and Dixie Lee Isaacson.

Special instrumental accompanists include Martha Pate, organ; Carolann Martin, cello; Mary Elliott James, viola; Arlecia and Secenia Scroggins, tambourines; Clayton Bohm, guitar; Michael Fischer, tuba; and R.G. Cook, trumpet.

Also performing will be the 48-voice Eva Jessye Concert Choir, the 30-piece PSU String Orchestra, a nine-piece brass choir and five dancers. The dancers are Kelley Coffman, Paula Curtis, Kim Graham, Rinda Gray and Joann Russell.

Following the 90-minute performance will be a public reception in the PSU Student Union. The program is presented in part by the Pittsburg Arts and Crafts Association-Pittsburg Arts Council, the Kansas Arts Commission and the National Endowment for the Arts.

In conjunction with the production will be a display of Dr. Jessye's private collection in the second floor gallery of Whitesitt Hall.

The collection includes costumes, scripts, musical adaptations, notes and compositions, momentos and photographs. The display will be on view through Oct. 13 in the gallery.

MAKERS OF THE SPIRITUALS

Makers of the spirituals—
A people washed marvelously with sorrow,
 swift to mirth:
Dawn was theirs, and sunset—all the colors
 of the earth.
The years gave them patience, anticipation,
Admiration for the prophets of old—and
 most of all—
Faith in God.

Eva Jessye (September 1978)

PITTSBURG STATE UNIVERSITY

Commemorates Its Seventy-Fifth Anniversary

With a Presentation of

Paradise Lost and Regained

A Folk Oratorio
Written, Directed, and Conducted by Dr. Eva Jessye
Based Upon the Epics of John Milton

Sunday, October 1, 1978   **3:30 p.m.**

Carney Hall Auditorium

PITTSBURG STATE UNIVERSITY

75th Anniversary Committee

James M. AuBuchon, Chair   Clifford D. Long
C. Ray Baird   Jack H. Overman
Kimberly M. Benedict   Betty Wood
Eugene H. DeGruson   Richard R. Carr
John Kreissler

Paradise Lost and Regained is presented in part by PAACA/Pittsburg Arts Council, the Kansas Arts Commission, a state agency, and the National Endowment for the Arts, a federal agency.

Other PSU Diamond Anniversary Events

Oct. 19, 1978	David Steinberg and Ray Stevens Homecoming Major Attraction
Oct. 21, 1978	Homecoming
Oct. 26, 1978	U.S. Marine Corps Band
Nov. 2, 1978	Romanian State Orchestra
Feb. 15, 1979	Kansas City Philharmonic
Apr. 16-26, 1979	Missouri Repertory Theatre

Paradise Lost and Regained: A Brief History

Sometime during his fiftieth year, in 1658, John Milton began work on his epic, *Paradise Lost*. The idea was not new to him, however; he states that the theme had a "long choosing and beginning late." Blind from the age of forty-four, Milton did not complete his work until some time between 1663 and 1665. Another two years were to pass before the long poem was published in book form, and still another four years were to pass before *Paradise Regained* was published in 1671. Milton died in 1674, and his epics were not to be in print again until the second edition of 1680, the third edition appearing in 1688. But by the Eighteenth Century, the works had become classics in the English-speaking world; they have been readily available in inexpensive editions ever since.

It was no doubt a school edition that Eva Jessye picked up in a New York bookstall around 1937. She took the volume to her apartment on 133rd Street, and as she read she recognized a parallel between the lofty verse of Milton and the simple words of the spirituals of her youth. Despite professional engagements, a move to a third floor apartment on 129th Street, and numerous other interruptions, she developed a thirty-minute oratorio for NBC Radio.

Numerous performances of the oratorio followed throughout the years, generally being presented in churches, eventually being televised by WBZ (Boston) in their Our Believing World series. In 1972 Dr. Jessye was invited to prepare a production for the Washington Cathedral. Extended to an hour in performance and incorporating dancers, the oratorio was a resounding success. In addition to Dr. Jessye's adaptation of traditional spirituals, it incorporated two songs of her own creation, "Lucifer, Son of the Morning" and "That Ancient City on the Seven Hills."

Pittsburg State University opens its Seventy-Fifth Anniversary celebration and the State of Kansas honors its native-born Eva Jessye with this, the definitive production of *Paradise Lost and Regained*. Since August 21, Dr. Jessye has been working with the personnel of this production, developing instrumentation, adding a "grass roots" version of "Go Down, Moses," enlarging a cherished construct to the production which you view today. It is with great pride that *Paradise Lost and Regained* is presented in the one-hundred-and seventeenth year of the State of Kansas, the seventy-fifth year of Pittsburg State University, and the eighty-third year of Dr. Eva Jessye.

Dr. Eva Jessye, born in Coffeyville, Kansas, on January 20, 1895, was educated in the public schools of Coffeyville and Iola. A 1914 graduate of Western University at Quindaro, she later was graduated from Langston University.

After teaching in the public schools of Taft, Haskell, and Muskogee, Oklahoma, Dr. Jessye became director of music at Morgan College, Baltimore, in 1920. Leaving that position in 1925, she served for a time on the staff of the Baltimore *Afro-American*. She went to New York in 1926 to study under Will Marion Cook and music theorist Percy Goetschius. By the end of the decade, her Original Dixie Jubilee Singers, later renamed the Eva Jessye Choir, were popular performers on both stage and radio, appearing regularly on the Major Bowes Family Radio Hour and the General Motors Hour. Dr. Jessye is acknowledged as the first Black woman to win international distinction as a director of a professional choral group.

The Eva Jessye Choir, with a repertoire encompassing spirituals, work songs, mountain ballads, ragtime jazz, and light opera, performed throughout America and Europe and served as singers in numerous Broadway shows and musical motion pictures, the first being King Vidor's *Hallelujah,* produced by MGM in 1929. Dr. Jessye has appeared in *Black Like Me* and *Slaves;* other motion picture credits include *Little Murders, Cotton Comes to Harlem, The Hot Rock,* and *The Confession of Joel Delaney.*

In 1934 Dr. Jessye was engaged as choral director of Gertrude Stein and Virgil Thomson's *4 Saints in 3 Acts.* A year later she was chosen by George Gershwin to direct the chorus of *Porgy and Bess.* She was associated with virtually every professional production of this opera until 1958 and is currently writing a book of the opera's performance history.

Devoted to the cause of racial equality and understanding, Dr. Jessye participated in Martin Luther King's historic Civil Rights March on Washington in 1963, the Eva Jessye Choir being designated by Dr. King as the official choir.

Dr. Jessye has established the Eva Jessye Afro-American Music Collection at the University of Michigan, Ann Arbor, and the Eva Jessye Collection at Pittsburg State University.

Dr. Jessye has received numerous honorary degrees from leading colleges and universities throughout the country, including Wilberforce University and Allen University. She is a member of ASCAP, the Negro Actor's Guild, and Sigma Gamma Rho Sorority.

PARADISE LOST AND REGAINED: A FOLK ORATORIO

Libretto: John Milton Music: Eva Jessye

The Father.....Robert Docherty The Son.....Robert Smith Satan.....James Mosher
First Narrator.....Charles Cagle Second Narrator.....Gene DeGruson

Elegy from <u>Serenade for Strings</u> (Tchaikovsky).....String Orchestra; Carolann Martin, Conductor
O Paradise, O Paradise (Barnby).....Brass Choirs I and II
Look Away in the Heavens.....Choir
Processional from <u>Die Meistersinger</u> (Wagner).....Angelic Host; Martha Pate, Organ
Way up in Heaven.....Carol Cook
Lucifer, Son of the Morning (Jessye).....Mel Bowie
War Between Good and Evil.....Choir
Ride up in the Chariot.....Choir
Palms of Victory.....Choir
Way up in Heaven.....Carol Cook
The Creation.....Becky Schwenke, Mary Elliott James, Joella Bowie, Pam Rexwinkle, Gwyn Bradley, Donna Randgaard, Vinita Hampton, Jennifer Parker James, Mary Helen Sherwin
Way Back Yonder When the World Began.....Bonnie Poulos
God's Voice.....Robert Docherty
Trouble in the Garden.....Irelene Swain
Way up in Heaven.....Carol Cook
The Son's Offer: Prepare Me a Body.....Robert Smith; Carolann Martin, Cello; Mary Elliott James, Viola; Douglas R. Stephens, Bass
These Bones Shall Rise Again.....Robert Smith; Carolann Martin, Cello; Mary Elliott James, Viola; Douglas R. Stephens, Bass
Praise Sequence: Honor; Glory and Honor.....Choir
Eli (Elijah).....Ruby C. Stewart, Arlecia Scroggins and Choir
Noah and the Ark.....Robert Moore and Choir
Father Abraham.....Men's Chorus
Go Down, Moses (Grass Version, researched by Charles Holmes, Rust College).....Robert Moore
When Moses Smote the Water (from Jessye's <u>My Spirituals</u>).....Burton Parker; Carolann Martin, Cello
Canaan's Happy Land.....Choir; Arlecia and Secenia Scroggins, Tambourines
Mount Sinai.....Choir; Arlecia and Secenia Scroggins, Tambourines
Tabernacle.....Vinita Hampton, Dixie Lee Isaacson, William Vance, Burton Parker, James Kindall
Joshua Fought the Battle of Jericho.....James Kindall and Lemuel Sheppard; Michael Fischer, Tuba; R. G. Cook, Trumpet
David Was a Shepherd Boy.....William Vance with Joyce Medford, Carol Cook, Mary Helen Sherwin, Arlene Stephan, Ann Kosch, Janeil Bryan, Mel Bowie, Myron Higerd, Richard Carson
Now Daniel Was a Hebrew Child.....William Vance with Mel Bowie, Burton Parker, James Kindall
You Read about Samson.....Robert Diskin; Clayton Bohm, Guitar
Sinning in Zion.....Irelene Swain
Prophecy.....Dixie Lee Isaacson, Janis DeChicchio, Joella Bowie, William Vance, Burton Parker, James Kindall
He Went on Man's Bond.....Irelene Swain
The Son's Baptism.....Myron Higerd, Bonnie Poulos, Joyce Medford, Jennifer Parker James, Arlecia Scroggins
Holy Is the Son of God.....Vinita Hampton, Joyce Medford, Carol Cook
Jerusalem (O What a Beautiful City).....Irelene Swain and Choir
Rome (City on Seven Hills).....Dixie Lee Isaacson
Paradise Regained: He Is the King of Kings, Lord of Lords.....Choir
Ride on, King Jesus.....Choir

> "True image of the Father, whether thron'd
> In the bosom of bliss, and light of light
> Conceiving, or remote from Heaven, enshrin'd
> In fleshly Tabernacle, and human form,
> Thou hast regain'd lost Paradise....
> A fairer Paradise is founded now
> For Adam and his chosen Sons...."

Amen.....Choir

[Please withhold applause until the end of the performance]

PRODUCTION STAFF

Director and Conductor	Eva Jessye
Coordinator of Choirs	Marshall Turley
Conductor of String Orchestra	Carolann Martin
Brass Choirs Director	Gary Corcoran
Dance Director	M. Evelyn Triplett
Set Design and Technical Direction	Barry Bengsten
Costumes	Linda Vollen
Sound and Recording	Paul R. Lawrence
Publicity	Richard R. Carr
Stage Crew	Departments of Music and Speech and Theatre

EVA JESSYE CONCERT CHOIR

SOPRANOS
Linda Beckman
Gwyn Bradley
Carol Cook
Janis DeChicchio
Patricia Flagler
Vinita Hampton
Theresa Hosier
Dixie Lee Isaacson
Jennifer Parker James
Meredith Mizell
Deborah Pierce
Donna Randgaard

Pam Rexwinkle
Marva Screws
Arlecia Scroggins
Mary Helen Sherwin

ALTOS
Joella Bowie
Janeil Bryan
Eunice Finney Creitz
La Taunya Gaines
Mary Elliott James
Ann Kosch
Cindy Manlove
Bonnie Poulos

Becky Schwenke
Secenia Scroggins
Arleen Stephan
Ruby C. Stewart
Margaret Thuenemann

TENORS
Mel Bowie
Richard Clark
Warren Ellinger
Steven Finkemeier
Joe Ford
Myron Higerd
Rick Knight

William Vance
Marcus Wright

BASSES
Richard Carson
Robert Diskin
Derrick Hall
James Kindall
Robert Moore
Burton Parker
Kirk Pemberton
Lemuel Sheppard
Jeff Summers
Russ Vallier

PITTSBURG STATE UNIVERSITY STRING ORCHESTRA

FIRST VIOLINS
David Emerson, Concertmaster
Paul Carlson
Markwood Holmes
Kirt E. Duffy
Linda Vollen
Don Sieberns
Helen M. Worthington
Marilyn Layden

SECOND VIOLINS
Richard Clark, Principal
James Poulos
Secenia Scroggins
Scott Nelson
Amy Thompson
Deanna Knott
Patricia Flagler
Julia A. Truel

Joan Sheverbush
Nancey Wade
Carol Cook

VIOLAS
Susan Schinzing, Principal
Logan Jones
Mary Elliott James
Peg Varvel

VIOLONCELLOS

Michael Burton, Principal
Heather Williams
Becky Schwenke
Arlecia Scroggins
Eunice Finney Creitz

DOUBLE BASSES
Douglas R. Stephens, Principal
Marcus Wright

BRASS CHOIRS

Gary Corcoran, Trumpet I]
Don Rogers, Trumpet II]
Martin Zentner, Trombone] Brass Choir I
Gene Vollen, Baritone Horn]
Michael Fischer, Tuba]

R.G. Cook, Trumpet I]
Dave Smith, Trumpet II] Brass Choir II
Robert Kehle, Trombone I]
Bruce Dunfee, Trombone II]

DANCERS

Kelley Coffman   Paula Curtis   Kim Graham   Rinda C. Gray   Joann Russell

A Public Reception Will Follow the Performance in the Student Union

The Lowry Organ and Kawai Piano used in this performance have been supplied through the courtesy of Dale Connors of the Joplin Piano Company.

Acknowledgements: President and Mrs. James B. Appleberry, Gene Vollen, Gene DeGruson, James Aubuchon, Wilma Minton, Jack Overman, Larry Nokes, Rod Dutton, Judy Riches, Elaine and V.J. Emmett, Martha Beakley, Clemence DeGruson, Department of Printing, Pittsburg State University Campus Security First Methodist Church of Pittsburg, Pittsburg State University Duplicating Services Wright's Greenhouse

This program is presented in part by the PAACA/Pittsburg Arts Council, the Kansas Arts Commission, a state agency, and the National Endowment for the Arts, a federal agency.

ing ovation that lasted over five minutes. While expressing her gratitude, she injected a dialogue of personal humor between God and Mr. DeGruson.

The Dialogue:

God: I guess we had better go down and call Eva Jessye home.
DeGruson: No, God! Please let her come to Pittsburg State University on October 1. We need her.
God: I suppose we can delay the call for this time.
DeGruson: Thank you, God!

This produced soft laughter from the assembly.

We are most appreciative of the persistence, persuasion, and perceptive efforts of Mr. Eugene DeGruson, curator of Special Collection, Pittsburg State University Library. The Eva Jessye collection of books, music, poetry, and other mementos will be housed at Pittsburg State University Library, and a tape of the performance here will be played over the "Voice of America."

Summary

Some of the reasons for my tributes to the above-named artists follow:

1. Each individual became a success through persistence.
2. Great self-sacrifice was the key that opened the door to their achieving success.
3. They all have two common factors:
    a. First, all are Afro-Americans,
    b. Secondly, their parents urged them "To embrace a better life," that is, always to move upward.
4. Tolerance played an important role in their lives.
5. They are proud to belong to the human race.
6. Every one ennobled the populace.
7. All set patterns that others could follow.
8. Each shared his talents.
9. They were Christians.
10. All displayed stamina in times of stress and rejection.